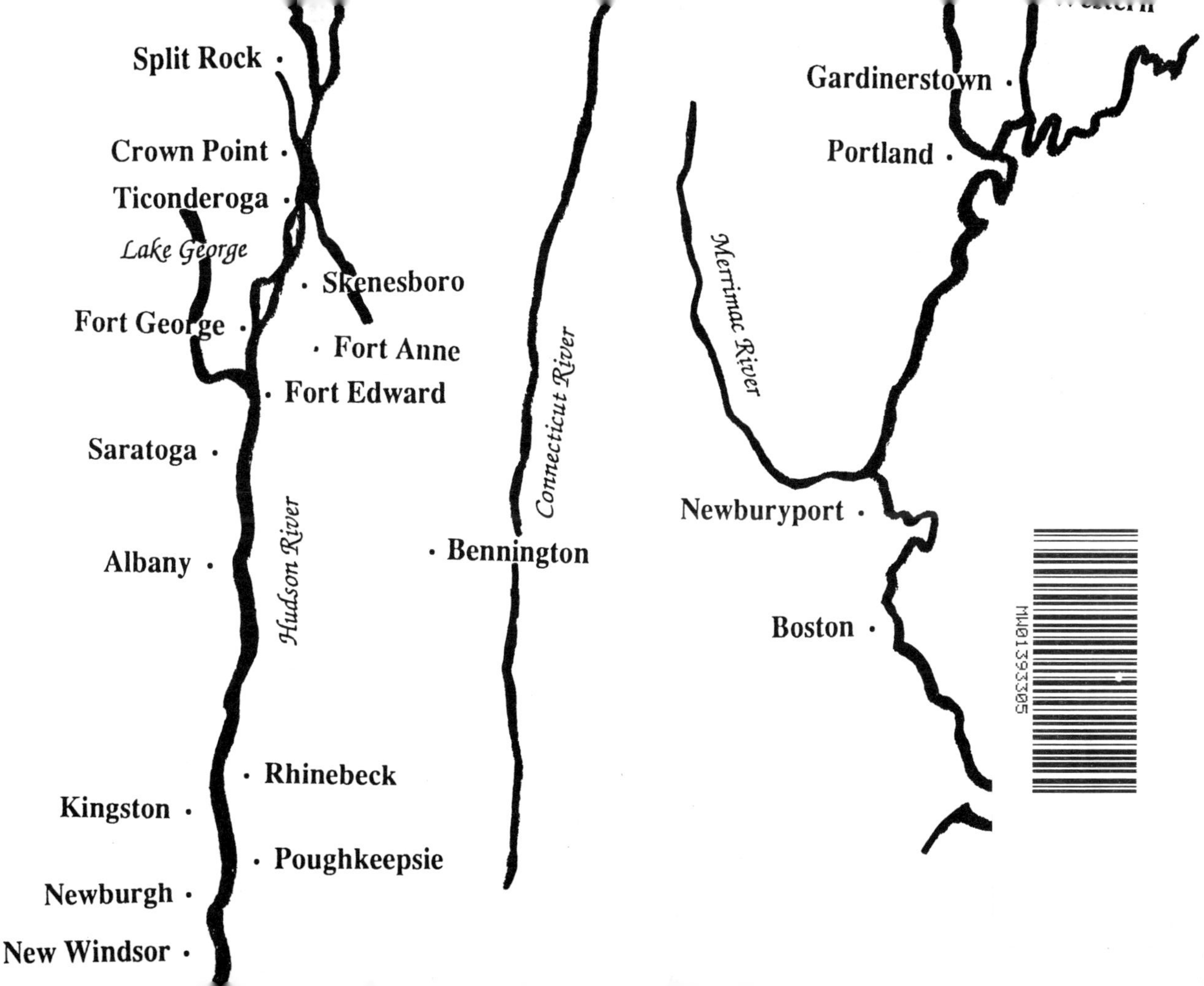
Split Rock
Crown Point
Ticonderoga
Lake George
Skenesboro
Fort George
Fort Anne
Fort Edward
Saratoga
Albany
Hudson River
Connecticut River
Bennington
Rhinebeck
Kingston
Poughkeepsie
Newburgh
New Windsor
Merrimac River
Gardinerstown
Portland
Newburyport
Boston

The Arnold/Andre Transcripts:
A Reconstruction

Benjamin Franklin's "Plan of Union" for the colonies was presented at the Hartford Convention. This cartoon was drawn to suppport that plan and is believed to be the first cartoon to appear in a newspaper.

Other Works by:

Craft Technical Writing
College English
Hugh Henry Brackenridge
A Hugh Henry Brackenridge Reader
Incidents of the Insurrection
Exiles at Home
Spectrum of Rhetoric

The Arnold/Andre Transcripts:
A Reconstruction

by
Daniel Marder

Library Research Associates Inc.
Monroe, New York
1993

©Copyright
1993
Daniel Marder

Printed in the United States of America. Except as permitted under the United States Copyright Act of 1976, no part of this publication may be reproduced, distributed, or stored in a database or retrieval system without prior written permission of the publisher.

Library Research Associates, Inc.
Dunderberg Road, RD#5, Box 41
Monroe, New York 10950

Library of Congress Cataloging-in-Publication Data:

Marder, Daniel (1923 -   )
    The Arnold / Andre Transcripts: A Reconstruction by Daniel Marder
    205p.
    Includes bibliographical references.
    ISBN:0-912526-59-9 : $21.00
    1. United States -- History -- Revolution. 1775-1783 -- Fiction. 2. Arnold, Benedict, 1741-1801 -- Fiction. 3. André, John, 1751-1780 -- Fiction. I. Title.
PS3563.A64417A89   1993
813'.54--dc20   92-46364
                                                                      CIP

Dedication

for
Roberta

Table of Contents

Preface ix
Acknowledgments xi
Introduction xiii
1. A Smuggler's Log - *Mihi Gloria Suram* 1
   1763-1775
2. Chronicle of the Cathedral Close 25
   1769-1770
3. Regimental Memorandum Book: Ticonderoga . . 39
   1775
4. Narrative of Canada and Captivity 61
   1775
5. Journal of the Wilderness March 79
   1775
6. Notes on the Siege 101
   1775-1776
7. Reflections on Montreal and Valcour 115
   1776
8. Letter to Anna Seward 125
   1778
9. Battles of Freeman's Farm: 135
   A Memorial by a Participant 1777
10. Observations En Route to New York 151
    1778
11. Manuscript Book of Intelligence 157
    1780
12. Record of the Court of Inquiry 183
    1780
Bibliography 201

Preface

The name Benedict Arnold is universally despised. It is synonymous with treason and evokes emotion usually reserved for the treacherous. But the memory of Arnold's co-conspirator, John Andre, arouses softer passions. Execution of the poetic and boyish adjutant general of the British Army was unbearable to the man who ordered it. The windows of Washington's headquarters looking out upon the hanging hill were shuttered against the rattle of the drums.

Both men, contrapuntal personalities, were driven by irrepressible ambition which culminated in the fateful conspiracy. It came within a hairsbreath of thwarting the American Revolution.

In twelve recovered documents, the conspirators reveal their dramatic natures and the events leading to the catastrophic moment. The transcripts may serve to shatter traditionally accepted myths of treason.

In the first, "A Smuggler's Log," we hear Arnold's bombastic voice from the New Haven jail where he is held for debt. He reveals events of his headstrong childhood, his apprenticeship, and his career as respected apothecary, husband, militia captain, and runner of contraband. In the second, we hear John Andre's effete account of his alliances in the cathedral close of Lichfield, England. Both are merchants ambitious for glory; each narrative ends in a march to war. The third transcript renders Arnold's clash with Ethan Allen over the command of troops at Ticonderoga.

These are followed by Andre's disturbing entrance on the confused American scene, his flight to Canada and his capture there. In captivity Andre hears of Arnold's Hannibal-like exploits, which ironically provide the means of his release. This is the "Wilderness March" which Arnold renders in the next transcript, followed by his siege of Quebec and his reflections on the betrayals and slights he endures after he is wounded and is recuperating in Montreal.

Soon Arnold is building a fleet and sails up Lake Champlain for another bout with the British. He loses this fight but consoles himself that he chased the enemy back to Canada, giving Washington a year's time to recoup his army. Arnold is too rash, making numerous personal enemies. He is saved from a court's condemnation only because his commander, Horatio Gates, needs his dash and verve.

Next is a letter Andre sends his poetic confidente, Anna Seward, regretting the death of one Honora, who jilted him in Lichfield, after which he joined the British army. The letter recounts Andre's enormous enjoyment of the British occupation of Philadelphia and the culmination of that delightful time in a huge celebration which Andre helped design to honor his departing General Howe. The letter reveals his attachment to Peggy Shippen. Unfortunately she also prefers the confidente's roll. The transcript immediately following places us in the midst of the greatest battle of the war, Saratoga (actually the battles at Freeman's Farm), seen through Arnold's incensed sensibility, "by a participant." This participant feels much abused by his commander, Horatio Gates.

Again we march with Andre as the British abandon Philadelphia to the American rebels who are to be led by Arnold, the new military governor. He is reviled by the town leaders. The eleventh transcript is Major Andre's "Manuscript Book of Intelligence," where we learn that Arnold, now a widower, meets and marries the 20-year-old Tory belle, Peggy Shippen. Andre describes the treason step by step as Mrs. Arnold manipulates it and as he and Arnold plot and enact it. The final transcript is the "Record of the Court of Inquiry." Here we discover what actually happened, how Andre is captured and hung, and how Arnold escapes to *The Vulture*, British man-of-war.

Daniel Marder
May 1993

Acknowledgments

These imaginative reconstructions are faithful to the historical record. They elaborate upon materials found in depositories like the Clements Library at the University of Michigan, the British Museum Library, the Library of Congress, and the New York Public Library. The staffs of these institutions have been invaluable in this work. I am also indebted to the International Library Loan Service for copies of rare records of court proceedings, memoirs, journals, and newspapers. Sources I have consulted include biographies, fictions, histories, journals, and unpublished documents, as listed in the bibliography.

Introduction

Major John Andre was caught in a plot with General Benedict Arnold to surrender West Point to the British. Hung as a spy on October 2, 1780, Andre's belongings were sent to Sir Henry Clinton, Supreme Commander of the British forces in America. With one exception, Andre's letters, journals and other papers represented in this collection were discovered in Gibraltar where Sir Henry died as governor on December 23, 1795. The exception is an account of his youthful enthusiasms which lay among the papers of Anna Seward at Lichfield, England.

Manuscripts of Benedict Arnold — letters, logs, memoranda — were found among papers confiscated from his home in Philadelphia upon discovery of the West Point conspiracy. Eventually they were returned to his family in England who suppressed them, fearing the universal abhorrence of a traitor.

The last item in this collection is the Record of the Court of Inquiry which condemned Andre to the gibbet.

Pages too withered and water-stained to be readable have been excised and the text has been edited for coherence and more sprightly reading. Titles have been supplied for some manuscripts.

Colonel Benedict Arnold

Chapter 1

A Smuggler's Log
1763-1775
Mihi Gloria Suram

March 29, 1763
New Haven Jail

It is not money I crave, as my London creditors charge, but glory. *Mihi Gloria Suram* is the motto of our family, all I crave is glory. My purpose here is to defend my rectitude.

They were happy enough to extend the loans when I appeared in London dressed as elegant as an English peer and bearing letters from the Drs. Lathrop. I took every bit of credit they offered. But now rumor is about that I do not honor debt, and they scream, I am outrageous, audacious!

I was always audacious, a fright to the people of Norwich. Because of the strength built into my thick chest and shoulders, they called me "bull" (not bully, I protected the weaker boys). I was forever on stage, riding birch trees or hanging by a thumb from a rigging in the harbor. Companions cheered when I jumped into the churning water beneath the great mill, grabbed a slimmy wood paddle and hugged it to my chest as the wheel, trembling and groaning with my weight, carried me deep into the chilling dark, up into the wonderous blue, around, and down again.

Reputation is unshakeable. It hounds me still in New Haven though above my shop door the shingle states: "B. Arnold, Druggist, Bookseller, etc. From London. *Sibi Totique,*" which means, for himself and all. The shelves are stocked with the finest English goods: every sort of exotic pomatum, cold cream, tincture, rosewater, salts and powders. The books upon my tables rival an education at Yale College, from the Hebrew Bible to Tom Jones. My elegant assortment of necklaces, earrings and watches attract New Haven's very best ladies. They call me Dr. Arnold.

My debt is not only for goods, but a gilt chariot, which has drained sympathies. It is said I detest paying bills; actually I delay only if a bright speculation is at hand.

By what right, I ask, are London creditors allowed to jail a citizen of Connecticut, a leading merchant conscious of his rectitude?

April 2, 1763

Reluctantly my sister has closed the house in Norwich (already sold for father's debt) and moved to New Haven to maintain the shop. It is the best arrangement. She still rankles over my treatment of the village dancing master, a Frenchman. I had suspected an attraction and rode over one day unannounced.

They were alone, taking tea in the sitting room. That Hannah so boldly encouraged any suitor was distressing, but a dandified Frenchman, a Catholic! I forbid him the house, then stormed out and began a gallup to New Haven, but a sudden resolve turned me about.

I listened at the draped window and heard the disgusting nasal voice. Beckoning a friend to beat on the door, I stationed myself in the garden with a brace of pistols. The dancing master chose to exit through the window, which so annoyed me, I fired, missing as a gentleman should. Hastily he danced over the grass and departed our lives forever.

April 17, 1763

Sheriff Sam Mansfield inherited this post from his father. They're an old merchant family, very respected in New Haven. His stone house is his jail where he keeps a good table. He used to venture cargoes — hoops and staves — with my father who was a cooper with trading ships before bankruptcy and the bottle consumed him.

April 21, 1763

Mansfield proposes a partnership. He'll provide the vessel and his credit for the cargoes if I'll do the trading. His eighteen-year old daughter lends an ear. The sheriff says Margaret appears more interested in the trader than the cargo. She is genteel in her chores, quiet and shapely but a sharp piece of goods.

May 5, 1763
New Haven

I am free. How sweet and balmy is the spring air. Oh for the billowing sails and the taste of the salt breeze! The Drs. Lathrop have extended 500 pounds so I can share equally with Sam Mansfield in our venture. This alliance with the sheriff softens the town's censure. Even Selectman David Wooster, dour merchant and militia veteran, smiled today in passing. But I am mad to be off.

June 1, 1763

Selectman Wooster is appointed Collector of Customs. He says the "relief of debtors" law freed me, but it is actually a consequence of good feeling at the signing of the French Treaty last February.

Whatever the law, Hannah settled my debt for a few shillings on the pound.

Wooster warns that his appointment signals stricter adherence to the revenues, another consequence of the French peace. "The Crown has increased the customs fleet to deal with these abominable Connecticut cargoes." He is ever so upright, among the oldest New Haven families, and a hero of Ticonderoga. He has organized a New Haven military company.

June 30, 1763

Hannah has agreed to remain, to look after the shop. "God in his wisdom acts in strange ways," says she. "I pray your bravura will not try me as it did our God-fearing mother." Except, she grants, "on Sundays, when you were pious for her benefit."

I was relieved of such piety when mother sent me to school with the Reverend James Cogswell, her relative in Canterbury. Instead of the Bible, he was ever quoting Shakespeare, especially the poet's contempt for vulgar applause, "voices of the greasy-headed multitude." Schooling with Cogswell instilled in me the disdain for low company. My most notable achievement was strutting on the roof of a burning barn.

Yellow fever struck Norwich while I was at Canterbury. Mother sent word that our whole family was infected; my two older sisters were dying. "The call to you is very speaking," she wrote in her brave sorrow, "that God should smite your sisters and spare you. My dear, fly to Christ! He only is the door. But I would not have you come home, for fear it should be presumptuous. My love to you — I have sent one pound chocolates."

"Thy will be done," was engraved on each tombstone with a winged head of death. I would not read it. Even to harbor the thought was cowardly submission.

She withdrew me from the Reverend Cogswell's when my father lost everything. Overextended, a sudden tide of failure swept the decks — the ships and Windward trade, the shop, even our house. He was to be found in the taverns. Our loss was beyond prestige. The extent of it was driven home to me shortly after mother died and just before he did.

Mother had indentured me to the Drs. Lathrop after I singed my arm, shooting off the old cannon on the village green. When the constable grabbed my neck to take me home, I twisted free, removed my coat, and swore I would thrash the lord himself if he got in my way.

Drs. Dan and Joshua Lathrop were cousins who had attended Yale College. They bought medicines and supplies in London and sold them up and down the Connecticut valley. At the time they had contracted to supply His Majesty's troops with surgical instruments. Any boy would consider himself fortunate, but I had difficulty apprenticing myself.

While I was mixing a ponderous medicine one day, Hannah entered the Lathrop shop, "Constable Turner came to the house just now."

"To claim it?" The debtors had given notice, and Papa was missing.

"He's found Papa. In New London."

Over the twelve miles to New London I kept dreading the embarrassment to come. Papa had been a town selectmen and my great grandfather had succeeded Roger Williams as President of Rhode Island.

Two merchant vessels had docked that day and the streets were full. I lead my father through the crowd, tied and hunched on a mare, his eyes vacant, my knitted apprentice cap on his head because he'd lost his hat. When I stopped to adjust his stirrups, some harlot who seemed to know him screamed, "The scum that's too good for us, look at him, the old drunk." He stared straight ahead.

As we passed the King's Arms, a withered cabbage struck the mare. I couldn't trot the animal; father would fall. We passed more inns. Vegetables and fish heads rained on us. By the time we reached the high road, my neck was freezing from the wet garbage. He was still clutching the pommel, shaking, tears streaming down his face.

October 5, 1763
The Grenedines

We are becalmed in heavy air and I take the moment to reopen this neglected log. Since the Treaty of Paris ended the war, we cruise unmolested among the Windwards. Every sort of sloop and schooner can be found plying these waters, among them our little *Fortune* (40 tons deadweight). It manages well enough.

Not inclined to revel with revenue officers, I discover numerous ways to quicken profits, sailing wherever a pound is to be made. We've two servants now, helping Hannah, and several horses. I've sent the agent, Mr. Hosmer, my plans for the great house I wish to build on Water Street.

November 2, 1763
Montreal

Paid dearly for this load of molasses. Since the end of the French war, too many New England corsairs are dealing in the Windwords, causing prices to soar and plummet. They shot up this month, but how long can I wait for them to fall? I've tried Quebec, now Montreal. Moses Hazen says I should have brought woolens and horses.

Hazen is a Jewish fur trader and artful meddler in British and French affairs, a gnomic creature with a week's red beard hiding his semetic nobility. He's become a most valued trade advisor, knowing the manners, religion, and customs of the *habitants*. I usually find him drinking grog in the English Coffee House with Thomas Walker, a fat crony with an angled nose from a redcoat beating for his French collaboration. Walker, a devout Catholic, has grown rich on Indian trade but is now an outspoken commissioner of peace, unlicensed. Hazen is the more appealing. His riches and properties stem less from furs than marriage to "the sausage," daughter of the *seigneur* Charlotte de Saussage.

Established as a member of the Masons, Hazen is among the few literate traders and reads Teutonic poetry in his great stone house on the shore opposite St. Johns. One evening I was invited to enjoy the performance. The fur trader dragged himself from window to window, staring at the icy river, as he spewed noble lines of grief. Strange that he should adore the voices that condemn his people.

As Moses recited the old war romances, my mind wandered back to previous days when still a boy...when I had run off to the Northland.

Twice, actually. The first time recruiters marched with their drums and fifes on the Norwich green. I was fourteen and got only as far as Hartford before the Drs. Lathrop showed their indenture papers and took me home. But when I was sixteen, the French and their Indians were besieging Fort Henry, and the Drs. Lathrop let me go, probably because the savages would sweep down on New England if the fort fell. On the march, word came that it did fall. Their Indians had massacred the garrison then fled back to Canada. Frustrated, without tents or cooking gear, our provincial troops rioted and deserted. They threatened to shoot any officer in the way. I struck out for home with a rusty firelock and a pocketful of parched corn.

Back at the Lathrops I was bolder than ever, probably because town gossips hinted I was a deserter. My pranks and skills continued to enthrall the boys, especially when they led to fights with the bigger ones.

Someone sprinkled broken glass in front of the Lathrop store where barefoot schoolboys passed. It was said I did it. I was grateful that the Lathrops had minds of their own. Instead of punishing, they rewarded me. I was put to sea aboard their merchantman to learn the trader's art.

February 1, 1764
New Haven.

Out of desperation, Parliament has passed a putrid law to buttress the old Molasses Act. Our increased smuggling has become intolerable, they say. The new act will provide revenues to offset the losses. Not content to quarter their troops in our homes, now they seek to confiscate our ships unless we offer tribute. None of us "corsairs" have the slightest intention of paying this duty.

March 25, 1764

Even Selectman Wooster seethes. He called a town meeting and allowed my friend, the "liberty shouter," Ben Douglas, to read the protest of the Massachusetts Assembly: "Imposition of taxes and duties by the Parliament of Great Britain upon a people not represented in the House of Commons is absolutely irreconcilable with their rights."

April 14, 1764

Douglas has been elected to the Masons which was organized in New Haven by Colonel Wooster. He promises to pave my way. But he also associates with the rowdies at Hunt House who call themselves Sons of Liberty.

September 21, 1764

Ben Douglas has succeeded. I now wear the mystic tie and hold secrets. "Is the floor tiled?" Ha-ha.

Fortune waxes. I've purchased a huge lot on Water Street and Hosmer has contracted to build the house, a magnificent mansion of twelve rooms with elaborate gardens. Already Hannah and I are planting apple trees.

Tomorrow Hannah entertains Madame Marie Gabriel, a milliner from France who has moved among us. She has invited some of New Haven's best, along with the Tracy and Leffingwell girls from Norwich. For my benefit, says Hannah. I've volunteered to fetch them in my new carriage. But my fancy is challenged by Margaret Mansfield who now pretends an air of indifference.

January 5, 1765
Barbadoes

Running "Connecticut cargoes" between Quebec and Barbadoes. Wine requires no stamps. I mark "red Claret" on the kegs of West Indian rum and molasses and trade them for Canadian pork.

Paying for tax stamps is a criminal, cowardly act. Wooster sells them and calls us "guinea-chasing corsairs." He finds smuggling disdainful, but admits it is in the hearts of Connecticut folk as much as superstition and religion. I see myself as a Drake or Hawkins of Elizabethan times. Smuggling is my patriotic duty.

Brave ladies of New Haven are hanging lanterns in their windows to guide our contraband ships to secret night harbor. Margaret refuses to join them.

June 5, 1765
Honduras

We are docked near a battered British sloop in the evening shadows of the Bay. A dingy has crawled over from the British sloop. Captain McCoskie offers a glass of sherry to all masters in the harbor.

June 7, 1765
At sea

Afternoon sky sunny. Sea choppy. Good headwind blowing hot in my face. And satisfaction. Alas, I've taught a Britain his manners!

Lashing our load of mahogany to the deck yesterday morning, my surly mate, Peter Boole, was glad to remind me of Captain McCoskie's invitation.

Mindful that I'd ignored it, I replied, "Had to spend the time haggling for this wood." Then I wondered what McCoskie might think. I rowed over intending to make a proper excuse.

McCoskie is salt of the empire, an old British prig. Suffering hangover, he held a wet towel to his head. I commented, "Rousing party," and suddenly he blasted me, "Go to the devil, you damned yankee! You're like all of them, destitute of good manners or even those of a gentleman!"

That curse riled the tenderest spot of my pride. Above all I am a gentleman. The only way to preserve my rectitude at that moment was a direct challenge. I've not dueled, but know the protocol. Having no glove, I clipped a kerchief across that slovenly face.

We met at six this morning on one of those palmy uninhabited islands in the bay. (As mate, Peter Boole was obliged to serve me, but I don't trust him and refused. Smythe, a common seaman served.)

Six husky seamen pulled McCoskie's longboat ashore, the captain standing imperiously amid them like Lady Britainia. Enraged, I cocked a pistol and shouted, "One aide, one surgeon, it was agreed!" His crew departed.

As challenged party, McCoskie fired first. I stood facing him, sweating in the cool air before the sun emerged. His bullet hit a tree. Intending my bullet to breeze by his arm, I mistakenly grazed it. His surgeon stopped the blood and dressed the scratch.

"Resume your position," I commanded the frightened old fool. "I'm ready to receive another shot." Audacity controlled my alarm. "But hear me, if you miss this time, you're dead."

Apologizing, Lady Britannia bent a knee to the ground.

August 10, 1765
New Haven

Selectman Wooster is not a landed aristocrat but one who calls himself a "legitimate" merchant (without sea trade). In fact he argued with his fellow merchants this evening about upholding the tax measures. Some, including a Masonic brother, even favor the rewards offered informers.

I might have escorted their prissy daughters to a dance or taken them for sleigh rides, but always felt their low esteem. Unlike others who carry Connecticut cargoes, I'll not suffer these blockheads to give me a moment's uneasiness.

October 24, 1765

Turkey dinner with the Mansfields. A bold table. Sam Mansfield is full of proposals, but none concerning his daughter. I'm sure Margaret's attracted, but why so insensible?

January 23, 1766

Had to wait for night in freezing sleet outside the harbor, then seek a safe port. Customs boats were swarming. The Townsend Acts are making contraband so difficult, they threaten our prosperity. They've increased the rewards for informers. More and more merchantmen are unloading under cover of night.

Paid off the crew, who appeared satisfied. Peter Boole was not. I ignored his unhappy grunt. He made a point to say he was leaving town.

January 26, 1766

Crewman Smythe tells me Peter Boole has appeared at the Customs House this morning, in spite of it being the Sabbath. He asked to see a Crown officer.

Told that business is not transacted on Sunday, he headed for the tavern. "I 'spect he aims to inform," says Smythe.

Boole's a headstrong stub of a man. I found him rheumy eyed, bustling with resentment, and accused him straightaway.

"That's a damn lie."

I rushed the sotted miscreant and dragged him through the tavern door. "Get your rotten hide out of this town," I shouted, "I mean at once!"

Checked the taverns this night. Smythe swears he's gone. I'm satisfied the stubborn fool's taken my chastisement to heart and left the town.

January 29, 1766

Boole's back. I gathered a few rowdies from Hunt House and spotted him before he reached the Customs House. We tied him to a chair, reminded him he was in the midst of committing a great outrage but I would be lenient if he signed an oath. He agreed; this is the oath I wrote:

I, Peter Boole, not having the fear of God before my eyes but instigated by the devil, endeavored to inform a Customs House Officer against Benedict Arnold for importing contraband goods, and hereby declare I justly deserve a halter for my malicious and cruel intentions.

I solemnly swear that I will never again inform against any person for importing contraband into this Colony or any other part of America; and that I will immediately leave New Haven and never enter the same again. So help me God.

He signed at precisely 7 o'clock this evening, and was to leave New Haven within the hour. But near four hours later, I inquired and found the fellow not yet gone. I then mustered another party from Hunt House, took him to the whipping post on the village green, where he received forty strokes with a small cord, and conducted him out of town.

February 8, 1766
Again he's back!
Colonel Wooster sent word that the defiant dumbbrave has filed suit with the Town Council. He and Selectman Enos Allen, a gentleman of reputed good judgment, are to settle the affair. Boole is in hiding and I am advised not to seek him out.

February 15, 1766
Wooster and Allen have issued their opinion that Seaman Boole was not whipped too much. They awarded him 50 shillings.

I have submitted the following to be printed in the *Connecticut Gazette*:

Query — Is it good policy at this alarming time to vindicate, caress, and protect an informer, a character so justly odious to the public? Every such action tends to suppress our trade, which is nearly ruined by the detestible Stamp Act and other oppressive measures.

June 3, 1766
The Windwards
Fresh breeze until 6 P.M. The remainder of the day blows excessively hard in squalls from south to west, and plenty rain, large seas.

First cruise aboard the *Sally*, half mine, secured by mortgage on the *Fortune*. I'm also eyeing another sloop, *Three Brothers*, this one for myself if Mansfield will loan me money outright.

My fortune brightens because I yet defy the customs fleets, while the others more and more cower in the harbor, fearing confiscation. At this rate, my trade may wax to the magnitude of John Hancock's.

September 10, 1766
New Haven
The hole is dug and the foundation underway for my grand house on Water Street. Hannah is delighted, and I am pleased. She has become good friends with Margaret Mansfield and approves my plan to approach her with serious intention, the sheriff willing.

February 22, 1767
Margaret is mine!

June 28, 1767
More duties. We must pay the Crown now on staples: tea, paint, glass, lead, and paper. New Haven traders are dejected and the merchants are boycotting British goods. Samuel Adams is come to New Haven and agitates for American rights.

July 10, 1767
I've just helped the rowdies at Hunt House plant liberty trees on Water Street, including our own plot where the new house is growing, and I'm joining in the bonfire tonight. But I don't approve of them baiting the Royal governor and badgering citizens in front of the Customs House.

Whatever joy I take in their activity is less in satisfying my principle than my robust nature. The Sons of Liberty are a mob of vandals: my inclination is to resist them. I resist what does not originate with me, but I cannot resist derring do.

February 4, 1768
Is it possible? Margaret says my touch has yet to arouse her; nevertheless she is bearing. I am to be a father.

June 20, 1768
New York
    These Sons of Liberty are savage bull dogs, rougher than our rowdy river-front boys. Since I've docked here, they've toppled the statue of King George on the Bowling Green, driven Rivington, the royal printer, to England and smashed his presses.
    Loaded with spavined horses, flax, barrel hoops and staves, we're off for Martinico as soon as the winds permit and the sea calms.

August 29, 1768
New Haven
    Another Arnold! My son Benedict emerged into the light of this world at six this morning, the sheriff and his sister assisting. He is a mass of black hair. Margaret already sees my strength in his tiny shoulders and my hawkish nose on his face.
    She promises to be more loving, but I'm not sure what that word means for her.

November 29, 1768
    Home again. I've discovered the cause of her coldness. Its my going to trade so sporadically. I've agreed to sail when winter breaks, return with the fall winds, and devote the rest to my family.
    Margaret promises to be warmer.

January 5, 1769
    Vicious gossip is destroying the peace and reputation of an innocent family.
    A Mr. Bookman, whom I've encountered in Honduras Bay, has strewn lies over New Haven that I kept bad company in Jamaica, drank myself senseless, dueled over a whore, and came home with the foul disease.
    Margaret is ice again. I'm to understand her thaw merely obliged me. She is bearing once more.

January 10, 1769
Mr. Bookman does not accept my challenge. I have inaugurated a slander suit against him and sent the attorney Elihu Hall to the islands for evidence.

March 2, 1769
Construction has resumed. The house has been delayed since the cold spell last November. It stands a ghastly skeleton, timbers, columns, and fluted domes like bones poking the sky.

Hall has returned with depositions so vague the suit was dismissed. Nevertheless I've posted the depositions in several conspicuous places, hoping to dispel the gossip, and refused Hall his fee. Now he brings suit. Attorneys are not my preferred acquaintances.

July 21, 1769
Quebec
Not the least syllable from Margaret in four months of voyaging. I am in the greatest anxiety and suspense, not knowing if my letters go to the living or the dead. I have written her from almost every post, appealing for a word of understanding. I do not seek sympathy. It is in vain.

Of most immediate importance is the cash I requested. Two of my sailors have informed against me. My cargo is forfeit to Customs and I am in danger of losing the *Sally*. Margaret knows this, but not the anguish I've gone through.

If a bond is acceptable on the assurance of Moses Hazen, I'm off to Barbadoes. But I'll await the next post before sailing. I shall be very unhappy if I have not the pleasure of hearing news of young Ben from my dear wife.

August 14, 1769
Montreal
A letter from New Haven at last, but not Margaret's hand. Her aunt writes she has birthed and wishes to name him Richard. My heart is anxious and aching.

October 1, 1769
New York

I am the most unfortunate man alive. Laid up in this provincial city with pigs running the streets, nursing a severe fit of the gout.

But I am not discouraged. I bear misfortune with fortitude and without repining, since the race is not to the swift, etc. Daily I see more miserable objects than myself, and perhaps less deserving of misery.

The printer James Rivington is returned to New York and sets up again with new presses and a royal commission for his *Gazette*. In Fraunces Tavern, they refer to him as "Two-Faced Jemmy" because his articles favor both the Crown and its agitators.

Ugly mood here. The Sons of Liberty planted a huge liberty pole to rally around. The Crown's Regulars chopped it down. Again they set it up, again it is chopped down. When the Regulars came to chop down a third pole, the Boys met them and they clashed. Fortunately, fists and clubs only...so far.

October 25, 1769
At sea, homeward bound.

Creditors are pressing for payment of the cargo confiscated at Quebec, and Hazen reminds me of my bonded obligation to him. He heard Margaret's father is wealthy. I have sent letters to all creditors requesting that my wife be shielded from their importunities. I must not trouble her or cause any uneasiness.

Paragraph after paragraph have been sent Margaret, some imploring her to relieve my forlorn condition with a word. But she's written only once and there have been so many opportunities.

How anxious I am to see her and be home with family and friends.

December 3, 1769
New Haven
Home, alas! But no comfort. I don't know what to make of Richard, so fragile. Ben grows apace.

April 2, 1770
St. George's Key
Large seas and hard winds have swept me into this island where I hear the astounding news of the most cruel, wanton and inhuman slaughter in Boston.

Good God, are Americans all asleep and tamely giving up their glorious liberties? Are they turned philosophers, waiting till we are oppressed and reduced to poverty?

I write Ben Douglas: "Why don't they take immediate vengeance on the British miscreants? Or shall we all see ourselves as poor and oppressed as ever heathen philosopher was?" But enough of politics.

June 9, 1770
New Haven
The atrocity — five Bostonians killed, including a black — has been digested, classified, even named like an item of dead history. Instead of the uproar I anticipated, the legitimate merchants of New Haven, including our most proper selectman, David Wooster, and my sister Hannah, calmly refer to the hideous crime as "The Boston Massacre." As if it were the "Tragedy of Richard the Third" just performed by the college players. My blood boils freshly at such acceptance. "God in his wisdom," Hannah says, "acts in strange ways." It is betrayal.

July 11, 1770
Selectman Wooster drills his military company on the green, but docily. Douglas wishes to raise our own footguards; I have no time just now, having, first, to lift a great burden of debt.

The house is proceeding. I have altered the plan to allow for a personal shoe closet, also a larger coach house and stable.

November 2, 1770
At sea.
Trade thrives. I am cruising far and wide, from the sunny Sugar Isles to the frigid St. Lawrence. The Jacques and Pierres are smiling at Parliament's recent gift, the Quebec Act, while Protestant's frown. This Popish Act restores the feudal land laws favoring Catholic *seigneurs*. Moses stands with the priests, half-heartedly.

December 12, 1770
New Haven
The village is outraged at the death of Christopher Snyder in Boston. The boy was shot while I was still at sea.

Ben Douglas tells me it is the fault of a merchant who defiantly advertised to sell tea with the stamps clearly affixed to the boxes. A crowd gathered, shouted insults, and hailed mud and stones on a neighboring merchant seeking to dispel them. In much fear, the merchant seized a gun and fired, killing the lad.

Once more I ask why we set on our arses and do not punish miscreants who oppose popular will?

August 15, 1771
A few shingles may still be missing but I can't wait. Hannah and I are moving in. The fireplaces are tall with husky mantles. Elegant oak paneling throughout. Two wine closets. A profusion of flowers along the gravelled walks from the seeds Hannah planted this Spring.

October 1, 1773
Montreal
Opening this log after so long is like visiting the family graveyard. I abandon the comfort of my lavish house to voyage hither and yon, catching quid and feeding my creditors...while my countrymen riot in outrage.

John Hancock's sloop, *Liberty*, has been confiscated, but not without a tousle. A melee broke out when the *Liberty* was made fast to a British war vessel in the harbor. Enflamed by this emblem, the gathered crowd went wild in the torchlight, attacking the redcoats without regard to their bayonets.

"Publican" Sam Adams harangues up and down New England for the cause of colonial independence. Not even the mob at Hunt House would go that far. But outrage can unbalance the best of minds. What? Do I hear a feeble protest from our pompous selectmen?

Why can't I give up this clandestine voyaging? I steal through the night like a thief while my innards urge me to noble action in the cause. But what is that? Surely not the abominable treason Adams advocates; no, it is the restoration of our rights as American sons of Britain!

May 1, 1774
New Haven

General Gage has closed the Boston port. He blames the skirmishes between Crown Regulars and provincials which have been constant since January when John Adams "Mohawks" strewed Dorchester Beach with the finest Bohea tea.

Tavern talk is that both Adamses and Dr. Joseph Warren are gathering cannon and ball.

I'll not go back to sea. Fortune has been too generous to try her further, not while these provinces are awakening to action.

June 2, 1774

Sheriff Mansfield has leased his house and installed himself in a corner bedroom overlooking the port. Hannah is disturbed; Margaret content.

The old man is interesting company, knows science, history, military and other, and is sympathetic to the patriot cause (that's what they're calling it). And he's friends with the best families. Invites them freely to adorn this huge house and partake of our table (usually nine kinds of meat are served with Spanish wine, popes of it in the cellar), but few come.

August 3, 1774

The Reverend Dr. Samuel Peters, driven from Windham for a Tory and unwelcomed in several other places, sought protection in the house of the Reverend Dr. James Hillhouse, and was refused. Hillhouse is himself in need of protection "from the mobs of Wooster and Arnold," as he said. To be linked with Colonel Wooster is inspiring.

August 4, 1774

Hot and sticky, bugs swarming.

Maybe all clergymen are Tories. But the Reverend Dr. Hubbard shows more crust than his fellow religionist. Hubbard accepted Peters' promise to pay all damages from any violence, sent his wife and children to neighbors, and took in the harassed and frightened clergyman. They barricaded the gates, secured the shutters, gathered firearms, charged them, and sat back to wait.

The vote at Hunt House was unanimous — chase the Tory back where he came from. We arrived about ten and held our torches high before the locked gates, not knowing just what to do. Some hurled their bodies against the gate, amid shouts of encouragement. It was a leaderless vacuum. Taking charge, I shouted, "Dr. Peters, open this gate!"

The doorway cracked and the bent figure of Dr. Hubbard appeared, pointing a musket. "That gate shall not be opened this night on pain of death." The voice had the resonance of a bell.

My rowdies roared, demanding that I break down the gate. One hands me an axe.

"Arnold!" Hubbard's voice was commanding. "So sure as you break through that gate, I'll blow your brains out, and all that enter here tonight."

Old Hubbard has the reputation of a hard Christer, good as his promise. The axe fell to my side. "I fear no one, but I'm not a fool." I felt the boys' disappointment, "We all know

Hubbard's true to his word, and I have no wish for death at present."

My riotous crew dissipated, each going off at his own pace and direction.

December 28, 1774

Gentlemen of influence and respectability have formed the Second Company of the Governor's Foot Guard. My military bearing has so impressed them, I am elected Captain. This, in spite of my fiasco with the rowdies at Reverend Hubbard's.

Sheriff Mansfield, pondering why I've left the sea, says glory's my ailment, Mars my calling.

March 13, 1775

I shout orders to sixty-five sons of families who have snubbed me. They study the military manual and strut on the green. I'm paying for their uniforms: scarlet coats; lapels, cuffs, and collars of buff trimmed with silver buttons; white linen vests, breeches and stockings; black half leggings; and fashionable ruffled shirts.

April 20, 1775

British Regulars have exchanged fire with farmers at Concord and at Lexington. We are prepared, and just in time.

"It will be expedient," reads the Boston messenger on the village green, "for every man to go who is fit and willing."

Selectmen hurrying to the town meeting have to dodge my volunteers marching to our muster on the green. They've voted neutrality and appointed a committee under Colonel Wooster to make sure no warlike action is taken.

"The Crown has erred" the old coot declares, "We demand correction, redress of grievances, abolition of these intolerable taxes, but not the shedding of a brothers' blood."

Is he deaf and blind? It's war, by god!

April 21, 1775

Final muster on the green for our march to join the Continental army in Cambridge. Most of our Foot Guard have elected to go but some cavil and cower. They agree our cause is just but claim loyalty to the Crown.

And who disclaims loyalty? We march to assert our rights, I say, as British subjects.

Students have volunteered to replace the faint-hearted. Their garb discolors our uniformed ranks.

I have composed a pledge for all who have elected to march, swearing to conduct ourselves decently and inoffensively; to obey all rules and regulations, to avoid drunkenness, gaming, profanity, and every other vice; to obey all orders not enforced by blows; and to expell incorrigible persons as unworthy of so great and glorious a cause.

We are sixty strong and all sign enthusiastically, none questioning a word.

Jonathan Edwards, pastor of Yale College, sends us off with an impassioned oration, all of New Haven cheering us amid flying colors and the playing of fife and drum, all except the selectmen who meet again.

Doublequick to the town powder room. We find it locked. Then to the tavern where the selectmen sit. Colonel Wooster comes out.

"I request the keys to the powder room."

"You act in great haste, Mr. Arnold." I am annoyed that he avoids my new military title. "It would be wise for all of us to await regular orders."

"We're already marching. Regular orders be damned."

Wooster's dander rises. "I say you wait for an official summons from Cambridge."

I rage, "None but the Almighty God will prevent my marching!"

The Colonel is rigid as a soldier at attention, waiting for my temper to cool.

My decision is quick. "Either you unlock that magazine within the next five minutes, or I'll kick in the door."

A Smuggler's Log 1763-75

Colonel Wooster returns to his council. The sixty of us wait in silence until the tavernkeep emerges and hands me the powder room key. A great huzzah!

Pouches and powderhorns filled, we sing liberty songs as we march to Cambridge on the Old Post Road.

Farmers at Lexington fire at British troops when ordered to disperse. Eight Patriots killed, two wounded.

Major John André
From a self-portrait by André.

Chapter 2

Chronicle of the Cathedral Close 1769-1771

May 15, 1769
Clapton
Clipped from *Gentleman's Magazine:*
Rug Merchant Dies
An emigre from Geneva, Mr. Anthony Andre, was one of three brothers prominent in the London colony of exiled Huguenots. Mr. Andre thrived on rug imports from the Levant. The family resides in the suburb of Clapton, having recently removed from quarters atop the Andre counting house in Warnford Court, hard by Throckmorton Street. Survivors are the spouse, Mrs. Mary Louise (nee Girardot) of Nimes, France; three daughters, Mary, Anne, and Louise; and two sons, John and William.

July 2, 1769
On Holiday, Buxton, Derbyshire.
Mother chose this spa to recuperate. The brochure claims that the Romans preferred its curative waters to those of Bath. Actually, Buxton is a poor stony town with decrepit facilities. Invalids are everywhere, leaning on canes, riding in chairs, queuing at the well to anoint their joints.

July 4, 1769
The arrival of the Canon Thomas Seward from the cathedral at Lichfield relieves my misery. Meeting the two ladies in his

train I spouted, "Bright coals in the ashes of the ailing." One laughed hilariously; the other turned away.

The Seward family resides at the bishop's palace within the cathedral close, known as the resort of literary characters and actors. The Canon's daughter, Anna, is reputed as "the swan of Lichfield." She's a bit plump for the designation. Anna possesses a sharp commanding face surrounded by coifed auburn hair. Her father boasts she can entice speech from a mute. The other, Honora Sneyd, is the 17-year old ward of the Canon, and Anna's constant companion though nearly ten years her junior.

"The daughter of Edward Sneyd of Staffordshire," says mother. "When Lady Sneyd died, he dispersed his children among charitable hearts."

July 5, 1769

I lolled about Old Hall waiting for them, but when finally they emerged, one in a plumed hat and summer cape, the other in a bonnet and high waste fashion, they were gone before I could call out. They stepped into a waiting chaise and rattled down the stone road the Romans built to Derby. I grabbed a sketch pad and rented a gig.

The road jostled me over a moor dominated by cliffs and fissures, a country as barren as my future in the counting house. As I was passing the henge ("stone circle of the bronze age," said the brochure), I spotted the chaise.

Anna sat on a high stone, her plumed hat on the grass and her coifed head turned aside as if posing; Honora lay at her feet. "Miss Seward," I called, not unaware of my attractiveness and accomplishments. Affability never fails me. "What a pleasure to meet you here."

Again Anna laughed in her hilarious way. Then she drew back to appraise me, her eyes enthusiastic. "Candidly, Mr. Andre, didn't you chase after?" The rich auburn hair swept haughtily from the forehead. She turned to Honora. "You must be his object. I'm years senior to Mr. Andre."

The honied head lifted. Honora was blushing. I attempted an exchange with her eyes, but met a dull flatness. Could she guess at my wit and imagination? That I could extol her beauty in verse, sketch it, serenade it with flute, or guide it across a ballroom?

In a hushed voice the girl finally responded. "Might as well save his breath to cool his porridge."

July 8, 1769

Vacationing families aspiring to the same enjoyments tend to quick friendships. The Canon refers to me now as Cher Jean; mother and my sisters delight in Honora's grasp of *vengt et un* and faro. If she speaks little, the ward expresses herself winningly with the cards. She joins in Anna's peculiar laughter when I caricature other guests, and even hums to my flute.

Anna's conversation is an energetic stream of language and emotion, spiced with conceits and surprises. We've exchanged poems. She appears to know everything about art, literature, love, and virtue. What a relief from the constant talk on the Pavilion of boils and bunions or at the counting house of cargoes and pounds.

July 10, 1769

Anna gave me an ivory oval and asked that I paint a miniature of Honora. We sat on the bank of the Wye, pink and white philodendron reflecting in the water. Honora posed indifferently as Anna chatted and wrote on her pad.

With the bonnet removed, Honora's hair splashed over her shoulders like combed silk. When we danced in the ballroom, Honora's hair had whirled about her neck, the same color as the lamp light. Now the soft glow invited my touch, but her cheeks were less rosy, bluer, tougher. An indefinable trace of grit was there, as if some coarse glaze had been poured over Honora. Inadvertently I muttered, "A coarse texture will not take a high finish." Anna lifted an eye from her writing pad. "I mean to say I'm incapable of the subtlety this portrait deserves."

Anna leaned over to examine my work. "You have darkened the complexion." She observed the oval closely, than afar, then close again. "I perceive the painter in the painted." Her forehead furrowed. "Do you go about life enacting your own self portrait?"

"I must confess." I responded somewhat bewildered.

"I meant only that the two of you seem melded in the painting. But of course its unfinished. An old proverb says, 'never show half work.'"

"The proverb is from the Levant. Actually it says, 'never show a fool half work.'"

When Anna spoke again, she said, "Enchanting, Cher Jean," and she invited me to come along with them to Lichfield.

July 15, 1769
En Route.

Every turn of the wheel carries me closer. Soon I'll be one of them, talking poetry and art in the cathedral close. Anna mentioned the botanist, Dr. Erasmus Darwin, who judges her verse better than his own. Lichfield's famed natives, David Garrick and Dr. Samuel Johnson, had been schooled under Anna's grandfather. "He never taught a boy," she said, "but only whipped and they learned." Both are obliged to visit the Canon's coterie. "Dr. Johnson is not inclined to enthusiasm. Whenever he catches sight of me, he trembles."

Anna dozes in the seat opposite, joining the Canon in an occasional snort. When her lively eyes are opened I feel a rise of sentiment. Still, she has confessed to 26 years, and campaigns for the attractions of her ward. "A commencing woman who partakes of the angelic. She is more interesting than anything in female form."

"A perfect description of my dear Julia," I countered.

Julia was a pet name Anna assigned herself for the exclusive use of her Cher Jean. But it was clear. To be secure in Anna's affection, I'd be wise to attend Honora.

She sat, hands in her lap, looking out the carriage window.

"You are too quiet, Honora."

"I'm anticipating Lichfield." Her voice was deep-throated.
"You have missed it?"
"Not the people." She did not turn from the window. "Frightful."
We bounced along in silence. Canon Seward woke when our landau pulled onto the smoother road through Needwood Forest. He pointed to a stand of apple trees. "Those are my good green people." Honora was the first to see the cathedral spires rising over the trees and rooftops. "My ladies," she shouted, "My ladies of the valley." The spires' thin elegance deserved the title. Dutifully I announced, "I love them from this instant."

July 16, 1769
The Cathedral Close

The bishop's palace is at the heart of the close, a spacious stone structure whose residents live in proportion to it. Sufficiently beyond London to escape the terror of its authority, Canon Seward's coterie are addicts of Anna's sort of poetry. They praise one another for great authors. She's as happy as this belief can make her. We play instruments and dance on the clipped grass. We fence, leap, vault. Canon Seward commits verse to paper but his talent is for indulging the foibles of others.

July 19, 1769

Discussion tonight was dominated by Dr. Darwin, struggling with his words. The botanist is taken with Rousseau and is in the midst of a book which Anna has temporarily titled *The Botanic Garden*. He proclaims a belief in optimistic humanitarianism, which Canon Seward dismisses as humanitarian flatulence.

"The t-tr-true phil-lo-sopher is given to the st-study of c-causes and governed by reason as the C-Ch-Christian is governed by grace. He realizes all ideas c-come from senses, and st- studies the universe b-b-but without believing he will succeed in discovering its sec-crets. The t-true ph-philosopher lives in society and owes his overriding d-duty to society; he achieves pr-p-probity because he f-follows reason."

"Precisely," responded Canon Seward. "That is what religious education teaches."

Dr. Darwin insisted, "Religious ed-education t-teaches that humans have souls which must be saved. D'do animals also have souls?"

Anna took up for Dr. Darwin. With bell-like syllables, she completed what the imperfect master might have intended, "The issue is whether an animal has a soul as characterized by thought. Decartes, you know, argues against it. He is wrong, not for denying an animal a soul, but for allowing one to man."

July 20, 1769
Needwood Forest

The ivory miniature was a present to Anna; she gave me another oval and insisted I make a copy for Honora. We sat in Needwood Forest. The earth was moist, its smell blending with the blooms of flowering bushes. Again honey spilled upon her shoulders. The rosy patches of her cheeks were like paint against the chalky skin. More than once Anna had referred to her as a "silky angel." A white butterfly flitted among the blooms.

I asked if she appreciated Anna's remarks about the soul.

"I do not always appreciate high-minded chatter. I should think that butterfly more real."

The insect flew vigorously from flower to flower, totally insensate of the forest, the extent of the sky, the possibilities of pleasure. "In a day it will be no more."

"But now it is all energy. This is forever. The moth is out of time." She removed her shoes and rubbed her feet in the moist grass. "As I am." What childish artifice! Rubbish! But so self-pitying, I wanted to caress her, enfold her in my tenderness. "The moth is without color."

"White is every color."

"It is the cancellation of every color."

My hand reached out. It hovered within a breath of her shining hair. She brought it to the touch. I felt the silkiness, then slid down the curtain of hair to her shoulder, also silken. Deviltry glowed in her eyes. Sweet magic it was. I contemplated her small mouth, then leaned to kiss it, but her hands forced my face onto her shoulder; I could feel her trembling. She pressed me onto the damp grass. What role was expected now?

Her small breasts disappeared when pressed, I noted this from someplace outside myself, a detached observer, while the disorderly player inside awaited her exciting cues. She brought my hand to her lips, opened the palm and licked it, then thrust it inside her blouse. The points of her breasts were hard. I began manipulating them. Honora became unhinged, beyond all consciousness. Her body quivered and I felt a mound, my hardness rubbing against it, surprising and delighting me but dementing her. She thrashed and moaned. I observed my own thrusting motion, part of my mind wanting to free the hot protuberance from my breeches while another part censored the corrupt thought. The electric sensation absorbed me; I could not bear to stop. Then, heavenly surprise! I throbbed and gushed. Honora thrust on.

When her body relented, I wondered what to say. What was required now?

July 23, 1769

I have asked for Honora's hand and she accepts with diffidence. She is most difficult to reach since the event in Needwood Forest. But the further her remove, the more earnest my quest. Petulantly, she shunned the miniature ivory I finished for her. "Keep it yourself. That's not me."

July 24, 1769

Anna holds court in her dressing room. Only the elect are allowed. Honora calls it "the dear blue region," after the blue walls and delft tiles framing the fireplace. Bonds of intimacy are stronger here and she feels less insecure.

It is evident in the "dear blue region" that Honora Sneyd is the subject of concern and sentiment. John Saville, the choir master, is relieved that my proposal has been accepted. "I was convinced that you were devoted to Anna." He let me into a secret, "Two years ago, when Honora was fifteen, we almost lost her." He whispered the dread word, 'Consumption.'"

July 27, 1769

A display of boundless sympathy is the appropriate role. I pursue it to Anna's satisfaction. Profound sighs mark my solicitude when Honora complains of fatigue. She endures my attention a while, then stroking her hair, floats off to her room. To do what? Lay abed in her own fantasy? Once I confessed my military ambition to her. With dreamy eyes, she remarked, "Men are made for war and women for the warrior."

July 28, 1769

Canon Seward accepts my proposal with little more enthusiasm than Honora. He called down Edward Sneyd, who questions my ability to support his daughter in a manner befitting a gentlewoman in less than robust health. Did I expect the 5000 pounds, inherited upon my father's death, to last a lifetime? Not wishing to provoke romantic resistance, he urges us to avoid impulse. We might visit time to time, judiciously. But neither should dream of holy wedlock until Cher Jean proves himself as a merchant and assumes his position in the world of trade.

August 1, 1769

Cher Jean must endure an ordeal. He must win the dazzling prize by selflessly pursuing the trade he hates, must acquire the mein of a merchant and take his father's place at Warnford Court and the Royal Exchange. However painful, he must subdue all ambition of military glory. But men are made for war, Honora, are they not?

Anna promises correspondence on a high plane, while Honora, drooping beside her, complains of an ache in her side. "I'll be content to add the postscript," she offers.

September 1, 1769
Clapton

No hour of the twenty-four is so precious to me as that devoted to this solitary walk from town. But I am far from possessing the patience I evoke. Very short indeed was Honora's postscript. I am too presumptuous. From the little there was I received more joy than I deserve. This Cher Jean is an impatient fellow, but he will grow discreet in time.

September 10, 1769

My sisters are charmed with the packet from Lichfield. Mother is also pleased with the correspondence. It hurts her to witness my moods. The hope of another excursion to Lichfield could alone disperse my gloomy vapors.

October 5, 1769
Warnford Court

I no longer figure a merchant as paunchy, with a bob-wig and rough beard. Instead I envision a comely young man with tolerable pigtail wielding a pen with the noble fierceness of a duke brandishing his truncheon. A sumptuous palace rises to receive me; orphans and widows, painters, poets, fiddlers are encouraged under my protection.

And when the fabric is finished, my brain exhausted, I find John Andre on a stool by a small coal fire in the gloomy counting room in Warnford Court, never to be much more.

October 30, 1769

This morning is the finest day imaginable, the horizon not dazzling but a clear and distinct blue. The sun insinuates into the hills and woods, gilds the spires, and sweetens me with benevolence.

But such contentment is chased by the frightful news of the *canaille,* cunning and cruel peasants. Our trade is threatened. Yesterday a gang of angry seamen marched through Thameside. Refuse collectors joined them, and the coalheavers. Stages at Covent Gardens and Drury Lane are fenced off with spikes because of unruly protest over the high price of tickets. But what does it matter? Should my dear Julia and Honora care

> *If here in the city we have nothing but riot*
> *If the coalheavers can't be quiet;*
> *If the weather is fine, or the streets be dirty*
> *Or if Mr. Dick Wilson died at age thirty?*

November 23, 1769
Clapton

It is now seven and raining ice. Mother is gone to pay a visit and has left us in possession of the coach, but as for nags we can boast only two long tails. Sister Mary calls them sorry cattle.

My imagination paints a select few friends encircling the fireplace in the "dear blue region." What would I not give to enlarge that circle of friends grouped against cold, bustle, ceremony, and haughty censure. How long before that hearth will blaze for me?

December 8, 1769

None of us like Clapton. We chink glasses to the healths of our friends in the cathedral close. The draught seems nectar. So we beguile the gloomy evening.

December 16, 1769

Joy! Dear Julia invites my return. But no postscript. Honora has collapsed while visiting her sister at Shrewsbury. I am confident Dr. Darwin's skill and tender care will remove that sad pain in her side which robs Cher Jean of the precious note she would otherwise indulge him.

December 25, 1769
The Cathedral Close

New devotees are admitted to the intimate circle, an old pair of friends and a pleasing girl of some thirteen years with fine brown hair hanging in ringlets about her neck. Her eyes are obviously trained for sweetness and her voice for timbre. She belongs to Thomas Day, the taller of the pair, recently returned from Avignon. He has taken a house at Stow-Hill, next to Lichfield, and makes daily visits.

Day is ill-mannered. His presence in the "dear blue region" baffles me. His shoulders stoop, his face is pitted with small pox, his shock of black hair is uncombed. When Mr. Saville stared at his attire, which is suited to a country peddler or barnboy, Day explained proudly, "I am remarkably fond of wading in streams."

The other member of this twosome, Richard Edgeworth, is a red-complected Irish aristocrat meticulous to a fault, scion of Edgeworthtown near Dublin. To Anna he confides, "Lady Edgeworth suffers the want of a cheerful temper. Not happy at home, I am in danger of being too happy here." While Day and the girl walk over from Stow, Edgeworth drives up in a one-wheel chaise of his own invention. His mechanical genius compels Dr. Darwin's attention.

Meeting at Oxford, the pair remain friends through a love of books and a loathing of splendor. Day pretends to gravity while Edgeworth claims a constitution full of joy. "I am fond of all the happiness women can bestow." This said with an eye on Honora.

Posed like a self-advertisement before the delft-tiled hearth, Day enveighs against the "follies of fashion," fierce eyes below his raised brows also directed at Honora. But he admits weakness. "In spite of the evils women bring on mankind, they tempt my fate. I ever seek a female wiser than myself, who could ignore the vanities of her sex for the truth and goodness of mine." I note a deepening in Honora's flat blue eyes.

December 29, 1769

Not finding the desired object, Mr. Day devised a scheme to produce one. From a foundling home, he obtained Sabrina Sidney, the thirteen year old, and another, Lucretia, since discarded. He would rear them to his specifications and when they grew to womanhood, would select the most suitable to wife. In Avignon, ignorance of the French language protected them from impertinent interference. He taught them to read and write and imbued in them his loathing of dress, luxury, fashion, and title. But they battled constantly, cursing and tearing hair. Returning to England he found Lucretia invincibly stupid and gave her four hundred pounds to procure a husband.

December 30, 1769

Day's story has diverted the circle. They take kind notice of Sabrina without attributing any foul motive to Day. But Anna is shocked to learn that Sabrina's education includes the unexpected discharge of a pistol close to her ear and the dripping of melted sealing wax upon her bare shoulder. "He says Sabrina must learn self-control."

January 1, 1770

The girl is gone. To a boarding house at Sutton-Colfield. Day has decided she is too old to remain under his roof without a protectress. Honora is the focus of his attention.

Anna confides, "Few courtships begin with so little appearance of romance."

January 5, 1770

Tea in Canon Seward's library, Edgeworth, Anna and me. Edgeworth presented his friend's plan of happiness. "It is compatible with Honora. She's told me that Day is the first man who gives full value to her understanding."

"But does he value her character?" I was not certain I did.

"Let me say I feel genuine pleasure, even exultation, looking upon the happiness of these two people."

"Perhaps you should reflect," said Anna, "before you have cause to repent your role in this plan."

"Honora Sneyd is so reasonable and so reliable that if once she resolves to live a calm, secluded life, she will never return to scenes of public admiration."

"Are you speaking for Mr. Day?"

"It is his plan."

"And you have no reflection?...Is Mr. Day unaware of Mr. Andre's attachment?"

He pretended surprise. "From the attention and admiration he bestows upon you, I thought some romance might blossom there. You will remember assuring our friend that Miss Sneyd had no attachment?"

This revelation jolted me. Anna ignored my questioning eyes.

January 7, 1769
En Route

My abrupt departure did not much disappoint Honora. Acting as though nothing of a binding nature occurred, she admitted to an admiration for my talents, then cruelly informed me, "You do not possess the mind I require." Because I was not a warrior? Did she think Mr. Day — I dared not ask.

In parting, Anna said, "The dear blue region will be lonely."

"I'll not be going back to the counting house."

"I should have told Mr. Day that Honora was your—"

"Doesn't matter." Except that she has slightly betrayed me. "You are what matters."

Her eyes mellowed. "The affection between you and Honora is fratitude. Ours is a work of art."

February 10, 1769
Clapton

I am Second Lieutenant John Andre of the 23rd Welsh Fusiliers. Uncle David bought the commission through his influential associates. Out of the tight little world of Huguenot merchants, into the domain of steep British tradition! I will write Julia at once. Honora must know.

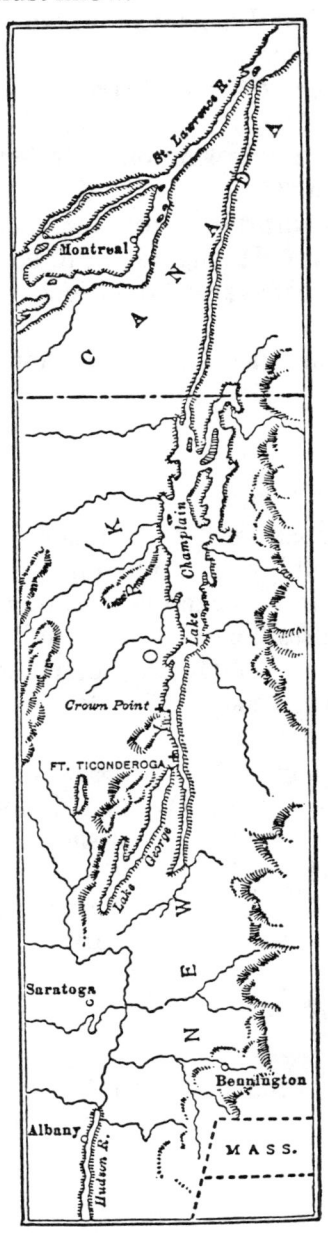

Chapter 3

Regimental Memorandum Book:
Ticonderoga 1775

May 3, 1775
Cambridge

Harvard yard was a Jacob's coat of colors: Pennsylvanians in chocolate brown and black tricorns, Virginians in white rifle frocks and round brimmed hats, Marylanders in green hunting shirts, the Delaware militia in ugly blue and red, Jerseymen in powder blue stockings and brass-buckled shoes. This crazy quilt stood out against a field of homespun and faded red coats that had been rotting in garrets and cellars since the French and Indian war.

My proud Foot Guards marched in to the drummer's quick tattoo, swinging smartly in the bright red and buff jackets I had purchased. We stomped through the stinking offal and rubbish, the pans, skillets and laundry hanging between the tents and the turf and sail-clothe lean-tos. The glint of our polished buttons and our disciplined march were so impressive we were appointed guard of honor to deliver the body of an English officer who died a prisoner.

But I was especially interested in attracting the attention of Joseph Warren, General of the Massachusetts Committee of Safety. It was said this eloquent defender of the Boston Insurrectionists had an attentive ear; and I had a scheme.

I began mulling on it soon as New Haven was behind us. Bright uniforms were not enough. I needed something to say for myself, some compelling military plan. At Hartford I sounded out an idea with a brother Mason, Colonel Sam Parsons.

As a trader, carrying horses and rum up the waterway to Montreal, I told him, I'd often speculated on the ease of taking the dilapidated fort guarding Lake Champlain. Ticonderoga is the gateway to the wheat fields and grazing lands of Canada. The walls are crumbling, no longer able to support the massive brass and iron cannon. As I bragged about my knowledge of the Ticonderoga cannon, creases in the face of my Masonic brother appeared to deepen..

"Not fifty men in the whole place!" Parsons blurted. Then his mouth tightened, his eyes narrowed. I realized that my idea had enough value to inspire a thief, also that I'd said too much.

No sooner was I quartered than I cornered General Warren, beloved everywhere for his support of the "Indians" who brewed tea in Boston harbor. He's a tall, heavy gentleman exuding innocence and virtue in spite of his foul-smelling pipe. "Ticonderoga can't stand an hour against a vigorous onslaught." I whetted his appetite with the prospect of seizing ordnance, and waxed on to include the capture of Crown Point as well, only 30 miles up the lake, then added a raid on St. Johns in Canada, where a King's sloop of 70 tons was docked. "Ours for the taking."

He let me know how very impressed he was with my acuity and military bearing. I sought action, not praise. Our meeting appeared so much wasted breath.

Late that afternoon, however, General Warren sent for me and I presented the scheme to his Massachusetts Committee of Safety. They worried over attacking a royal fort that had shown no hostile intention. An attack might be taken as more than protest, as outright war! And New York might object. Ticonderoga was in the province of New York. It was decided to query them. But my champion thought otherwise. "New York will deliberate until those cannon rust." The Committee submitted my plan to the Massachusetts Assembly where it was quickly ratified.

Within a week of my arrival at Cambridge as captain of the Second Foot Guards from Connecticut, I have acquired a trustworthy friend and am colonel in the Massachusetts militia. My Foot Guards are stunned, but I am not. It is natural. Nothing I ever do amazes me. With my assistant, Lieutenant Eleazer

Oswald, and a servant, I'm setting out for the Berkshires to recruit a regiment, not to exceed 400.

May 5, 1775
Stockbridge, The Berkshires

Punch, my huge Jamaican, wishes he could live forever in these placid hills of spruce and hemlock.

I am given a purse of 300 lbs., ten horses, and orders to draw blankets and tents, powder, barrels of salted fish, pork and flour as available. No pay is forthcoming. Temporarily, I'm to support the recruits as best I can, and keep an accurate accounting, Congress to reimburse me.

May 6, 1775

The hillboy would not enroll until I added more guineas. He asked, "Ever h'ard o' Ethan Allen?"

Allen is known through the New England colonies as a giant windbag who claims to be governor of "Vermount" as he calls the New Hampshire grants. He's a hard drinking freebooter with a price on his head for horse-whippings and tar-and-featherings. The giant leads an illegal band of 200 or so drunken, foul-mouthed mountaineers calling themselves the Green Mountain Boys. They're bearded, long-haired, tobacco-chewing skunks who by force keep New Yorkers out of the Green Mountains that are legally theirs.

"He and his war-whooping mob's already gone up," the hillboy continued, "aiming to take Fort Ti and Crown Point too."

Damn my unguarded tongue! I left the recruiting to Oswald and galloped north.

May 7, 1775
Bennington

A stuffed wildcat snarls atop a tavern pole in the direction of New York. The Catamount Tavern is Allen's mountain lair. Its a two-story cavern of a room with peephole windows and few lanterns. Tables and chairs are carved from logs. "Council Room" is scratched into the stone over the gigantic fireplace. A flabby slough-eyed tavernkeep confounds my uniform with the British. I show my Massachusetts commission and he tells me, "Parson Allen's on the march."

"Parson?"

"Fightin' Parson Allen."

"A powerful and fearless man," I say, seeking more information.

"I seen him tear a pack of cards into eighths and twist two-penny nails with his teeth."

"But I never heard he was so committed a Christian."

The tavernkeep shut down. He might have taken the remark as sarcasm and me for Catholic; my skin is dark and my features sharp enough. The Quebec Act, stretching Canada as far as the Ohio River and giving it over to French popery, had angered many a Protestant.

"I wear the mystic tie," I announced. "I'm a Mason."

He told me that Allen was bivouacked with his Boys and the gents who just joined his expedition at a place called Castleton, on the Vermont side of the water. "I'd say twenty mile from Fort Ti."

"What gents?"

Once I opened his valve, there was no stopping the flood. One of the "gents" was Captain John Brown, who happens to be a vague relative on the haughty Rhode Island side. Brown's a lawyer delegated by the Massachusetts committee to journey up the Sorel River to the St. Lawrence and sound out Canadian desire for independence. He impressed the tavernkeep as smart and genial, but possessed of a wagging tongue, "Bragged over much of his birth and schooling."

Another of the "gents" was "Fats," a fellow tavernkeep of Pittsfield named James Easton, talented carpenter, colonel of the militia, and deacon of the church. "Enough dry tinder in Fats," my host offered, "to kindle the airiest rumor."

The Catamount tavernkeep also confirmed my suspicions about Parsons. He'd come up to enlist Allen and his rambunctious

Boys, offering no pay but great reward from the Hartford Committee of Safety.

May 8, 1775
Castleton

The sun was going down in riotous color on the lake. Drunken war-whoops crushed the chirping of birds in the white oaks as I galloped into their camp before the Castleton graveyard. The war-whoops stopped; they reached for firelocks and tomahawks, rum sloshing from their bowls.

Allen stood with legs apart, a huge clown in bearskin hat and a greasy green smock. Oversized yellow epaulettes matched his trousers. Disdainfully he inspected my brazen uniform.

I produced my commission and announced, "By order of Massachusetts, I am in charge of this expedition to take Ticonderoga."

The Boys howled. They pranced and jigged, overcome with the farce that this popinjay in a pretty red jacket and traveling with a servant proposed to command hard-drinking mountaineers. Allen twitched his nostrils and turned away. Lawyer Brown, about my size and similar in build and feature, appeared not to know me. Loudly he told Allen, "The Boys would as soon club their firelocks and march home as follow this paper colonel."

Allen huddled with his lieutenants, "What'll we do with this rascal?" I was aware of the firelocks still focused on me.

"Put'm under guard." "Tie'm up." "Let'm perch." "Shoot'm."

"He's got a commission."

Official sanction tempted the giant. Accepting my commission, he could claim his venture an act of state. But Lawyer Brown was opposed. "Take his commission to Fort Ti and see how fast the lobsterbacks lay down their arms."

"I'll draw you a commission," offered Easton.

I shouted, "Its got to be official."

"This is a private undertaking," Captain Brown shouted back, "Besides, you haven't a single soldier to make good your boast."

Allen turned to Easton, "Go ahead, draw up a paper like his." Then he announced to the Boys, "In no case will anyone pay any attention to this rooster. No man's to heed any order from him."

I couldn't let them proceed without me. "I'll issue no order," I promised, "if you let me ride along."

Allen conceded. "Just stay out of the way."

I rode into the village and arranged an express courier to Oswald: "Hurry! Bring up whoever, whatever you can. Do not delay!" Riding back, I reflected on Colonel Parsons' treachery. To be expected.

May 10, 1775
Ticonderoga

We reached the cove on the eastern shore just opposite Fort Ti in the full darkness of night. An icy wind blew across the mile-wide stretch of water; rain lashed our faces.

"What the goddamn hell," Allen cried. Lawyer Brown had arranged for flatboats from Skenesboro to ferry us over. They were nowhere in sight.

The Boys grumbled and shivered in little groups. We had to cross before the sky colored or the sentries would spot us. I saw my opportunity and stole down the shore. Luck was with me. I returned, rowing an abandoned old scow. A second vessel appeared as the Boys scampered aboard. It bore a local, Asa Douglas, who got wind of our project and wanted to take part. His vessel was actually a barge commandeered from a Captain Black Jack. Kegs of whiskey were aboard, most welcome in moving the Boys across the lake.

A grateful Allen invited me to share command of the 80 or so Boys in the first crossing. Bitterly cold on the water, the rain turned to drizzle. Our scow rode low. All were soaked before we reached land about a half mile below the fort's stone walls. We lit a fire and were nearly dry when a glint of color appeared in the sky.

"What do you think?" asked Allen.

Surprised, I answered in a flash, "Attack before its too light."

Allen aligned his Boys in ranks and exhorted, "Each man marches because he wants to. Those not wanting, can return to the boats." No one moved.

I took a position at the giant's side and we began the trudge along the muddy shore line, a patchwork of buckskins, long frocks, and woolen shirts. Some wore bearskin caps like Allen's, but most slouched along in felt headpieces or no hats at all. They carried firelocks, swords, knives, pistols and clubs.

We followed an Indian trail along the lake until great and surprising works appeared, the old fort's contours looming in the breaking sky. I could make out a precipice; upon it redoubts, walls pierced with cannon. The path steepened as it climbed. Before the ascent, I claimed my rightful leadership.

"What do we do with this damned rascal?" Allen asked his Boys, but his voice lacked its usual timber.

I shouted, "Follow me lads!" and broke into a run. Then Allen shouted, and the race was on. Together we gained the height and rushed down the path leading to the wicket gate, happily open. A startled sentinel leaped to his feet, aimed his firelock, then dropped it and fled through the wicket. We charged after him to the inner court where a second sentry came at us with a bayonet, but Allen had him at swordpoint before he could bring it into play. The Boys swooped in. The wretched sentry guided us across the parade ground to a covered stairway, leading to the commander's headquarters. I gave an order to wake and disarm the soldiers. A mistake. The Boys ran through the dark corridors whooping like Indians at war, smashing doors and pulling astonished soldiers, woman, and children from beds.

Allen bellowed up the covered stairway, "Come out, you skunk, or I'll sacrifice the whole damned garrison."

A Lieutenant appeared, breeches in hand.

"No quarter! No quarter!" the Boys shrieked, and the giant screamed over the clamor, "I demand you deliver this fort!" He flourished his sword.

"By whose authority?"

Allen had nothing to show. He'd forgotten the fake commission. "In the name of the the great Jehovah." The lieutenant was perplexed. Allen added with increasing thunder, "And the Continental Congress!"

The lieutenant stood in his night clothes, clinging to his breeches as if frozen by awe of the giant in the bearskin hat. Beneath the stairway, a woman cowered with a child.

"I must have immediate possession of this fort and all the property of George the Third." Allen cursed and brandished his sword over the British lieutenant's head. "If a single gun is fired, I'll slaughter every man, woman, and child in this fort."

I countered Allen's rudeness by displaying my commission and calmly advising the lieutenant, "Come, you have no choice but to live or die. Surrender like a gentleman and you shall be treated like one." The Boys were tearing through the fort's bare furnishing. Captain Black Jack's whiskey was supplemented with kegs of rum discovered in the storehouse. "What can your drowsy fellows do against such madness?"

The lieutenant was not the commander as I should have suspected. All Allen's vehemence spent on an underling. A Captain Deleplane came forth and extended his sword hilt in capitulation. Forty-eight partially attired Regulars laid their arms before us on the parade ground and the crumbling old fort passed into American hands without a drop of spilt blood.

I did not object to the riotous celebration until I saw the plundering. They smashed what they could not lift. Screaming women were running in every direction, some clutching infants to their torn bodices. Several hilarious Boys pranced about with ribboned bonnets on their heads. Furiously I chased after, citing military law against plunder. One spit at my feet. I snatched prizes from their paws and returned them to the victims, until Allen, red and angry in rum, ordered me out of the fort. "I never agreed to a joint command," he yelled, then commanded Easton to read his counterfeit commission.

Shots were fired in my direction. A firelock pressed into my ribs, "Wanna be fired through? Or d'ya admit Allen's rule?" I stared into red eyes until my assailant lowered his musket and went in search of more rum.

May 14, 1775

Allen is a proper man to lead his own wild people, but entirely unacquainted with military service. As the only person authorized to take possession of this place, I am determined to insist on my right. I think it my duty to remain here against all opposition until I have further orders.

May 15, 1775

Allen has sent Easton and Lawyer Brown below, probably to stir resentment against me in Cambridge and Philadelphia. Easton is particularly despicable, a reptilian toady in a mass of flesh without distinctive boundaries except for his colorless clothes. His reddish cheeks and jowls are so fat, bones cannot be discerned. Nevertheless the face appears divided by the broad plane of the nose between the piggish eyes.

By contrast, Brown is a tidy and handsome fellow who studied law with my Rhode Island cousin, Oliver Arnold, and married the sister of Oliver's wife, so he is no blood relation, thank goodness. The pettifogger is a vindictive man, though I've given him no cause. Does he envy my quick rise in the military? Brown vigorously opposes my efforts to send our captured ordnance to Cambridge, which is the purpose of this mission.

Colonel Seth Warner, just up from Connecticut, tells me that Easton, who hung back pretending his musket froze while we stormed the fortress, has written the Continental Congress defaming me as a self-seeker, an interloper and nuisance in the taking of Ticonderoga for which he and Allen deserve all credit.

May 16, 1775

Crown Point is defenseless, having suffered a recent fire. The garrison are less than a dozen carpenters. Allen has sent Warner and a detachment of Boys to take the fort.

May 17, 1775

I was drowsing in my doldrums, frankly thinking of some paid relief with the strumpets who gather about this fortress, when Punch burst into my little cubicle, "Topsail on the lake!"

We arrived at the dock just as the schooner *Liberty* was mooring. As I so fervently wished, it bore Lieutenant Oswald and fifty attentive lads.

Oswald had confiscated the abandoned vessel from the Skenesboro shipyard at the bottom of the lake. I was delighted to find my secretary so resourceful and bold. Breezily he informed me, "Liberty Boys chased Major Skenes off to Canada with his wife, cooks, and slaves."

May 25, 1775

More men are attracted and join me every day, while Allen's party is decreasing. Disputes between us have subsided.

Berkshire boys make good sailors. They've done a fair job of caulking and mending the rot on this old boat, and armoring it with four captured carriage cannon. The Green Mountain Boys watch, wearing sullen frowns.

But Oswald proves a gillie after all, as his aspect indicates. He is palefaced, narrow shouldered, and displays the servile demeanor of a clerk. When Allen asked where we were headed, Oswald's compliant nature compelled him to tell. I've sent him below to counter the foul mouths of Easton and Brown who blacken my reputation.

We sail up the lake leaving Allen to his conquest, but the drunken giant is curious. He and his Boys have located bateaux and are chasing after, though none are experienced with the slow and clumsy flatboats. Tacking back and forth across the water, we never quite lose sight of them.

Seth Warner greets us at Crown Point and we wait in good cheer for Allen's exhausted sailors. We parley, tongue in cheek, before sailing on for St. Johns, about 80 miles distance.

May 26, 1775
Awash

The wind shifted from the north and the *Liberty* spread canvas. We vanished over the horizon as the Boy's struggled passionately behind, oars against the current.

But now we are becalmed, just short of the Canadian border. I've lowered our two skiffs and with thirty-five oarsmen we move like thieves in near silence through the channel.

May 27, 1775
St. Johns

At 6 A.M. we crossed the border and quietly broke out the rum to celebrate this first invasion of a foreign country by the United Colonies. In no time the old stone fort appeared out of the heavy mist. We surprised the watch, took a sergeant and his party of twelve.

The King's sloop has not moved from the docking where I had last seen her. The crew of seven surrendered at the sight of us. "Reinforcements are coming," their sergeant warned.

"And how would you know?"

"Because *Seigneur* Hazen has been watching your approach. He rode off to Montreal hours ago."

I crossed over to Moses' great house sitting up from the shore among apple trees. The servants took me for British. "The *seigneur* is gone to Montreal."

We laid hands on everything portable, stores, provisions, even cannon, destroying what ordnance and equipment we could not carry off. The wind springing up fair at 9 o'clock, we weighted anchor.

Renaming the King's sloop *Enterprise* and regaining the *Liberty*, I am Admiral of the fleet, first of the United Colonies.

We sailed back in quiet triumph, rowboats and bateaux in tow, amidst chirping birds and the sun gleaming on the lake.

A faint sound of churning water disturbed my serenity. It grew loud as we sighted Allen's weary oarsmen still in pursuit. When we were alongside the frantic Boys, I fired a salvo. They replied with a rattle of small arms. Smiling tolerantly at the mad fellows, I shouted, "We've rum aboard!"

Allen led the sweep across my deck and we drank numerous "Congress healths."

"Relief is coming to St. John," I warned. "It is a wild impractical scheme to continue."

"Me and the Boys mean to take the fort."

"We are masters of the lake. Why care about St. Johns?"

They jeered; my advice was craven.

In their hurry to follow, the Boys had come off without enough provisions or heavy guns. I had only food to give them. Then shrugging, I watched their exhausted arms pitifully thrashing to Canada and certain defeat.

May 29, 1775
Ticonderoga

This noon, my lads were refurbishing our fleet when suddenly they broke into great guffaws. Allen's Boys were tearing down the lake as if a British armada pursued them.

At St. Johns the exhausted sailors had fallen asleep in a field and were suddenly aroused by a discharge of grapeshot from six field pieces and the small arms of 200 Regulars. They scrambled to their bateaux, except three particularly sound sleepers who were left behind and captured by the British reinforcement.

I am reporting Allen's foolishness to the Massachusetts Committee, adding this note: "As to the calumnies and lies I hear being spread below by Deacon Easton and Lawyer Brown, to the effect that my real purpose in the North is contraband wheat and pork, may I trust the mouthings of tale-bearers will be given no credit? My conduct should not be condemned until I have opportunity to be heard."

June 1, 1775

We have received reinforcements but no funds. Now we are a hundred-fifty well disciplined men, exclusive of Allen's Green Mountain Boys who are drifting away by twos and threes, their recent misadventure persuading them they are needed on their farms. Seth Warner has conceded to my leadership and Allen has cooled but does not submit. His letters are still signed "principal commander of the army." The giant skulks with his remaining Boys; I anticipate violence before he is fully subdued.

My lads have readied the ordnance for shipment to Dorchester Heights. We await means of transport. I intend to remain here until the cannon are on their way.

June 4, 1775
Lake Champlain

Our fleet presents the best posture of defense, but my spirit is low. General Warren writes his suspicion that Easton and Brown, being Massachusetts men, are selected to undermine my commission from that province: "Easton complained to the Massachusetts Assembly that you have interfered with a successful campaign which was planned by Connecticut. And quite frankly the Assembly is only too willing to honor Connecticut with the onus of capturing two royal forts and raiding another. This is not unhappy news unless you are as mad as John Hancock and the Sons of Liberty raving for independence. Bolder than wise, we have gone too far." Bad boys, now Papa will punish.

June 6, 1775

The official letter arrived this morning, addressed not to *Colonel* but to *Captain* Arnold, denying the commission that has been my foundation: "As all our energies are committed to the siege of Boston, the campaign on Lake Champlain must be turned over to Connecticut under command of Colonel Ethan Allen."

June 7, 1775
Lake Champlain

Massachusetts be damned! My mind's afire with a dream of capturing all Canada. We beat up the lake in a small breeze, the lads edgy for not receiving pay, bound for hell.

June 6, 1775
Ile aux Noix

Scouts are out for all possible intelligence. As I suspected, only the clergy and the rich *seigneurs* are pleased with the Quebec Act; almost all *habitants* are disgruntled. But how many would actually rise up against the Crown if we moved in to support them? And will the Indians join us?

The Caughnawagas say that our transgressions at Ti, Crown Point, and St. Johns have alarmed the new governor, General Guy Carleton. He is arming the French, gathering troops and supplies, and threatening to burn Montreal if the lackadaisical merchants do not rally to the King's defense. All in all he can count on 550 Regulars and a scattering of loyal *habitants*.

June 8, 1775
Holiday Point

We are below the border again where Lieutenant Oswald rejoins us. He bears a packet from Massachusetts addressed to *Colonel* Arnold who is "much appreciated for his fidelity, knowledge, courage, and good conduct." Oh, and Massachusetts is hopeful that *Colonel* Arnold will retain command.

General Warren's letter explains that the blunt rejoicing of the people over the capture of Fort Ti has charged the atmosphere. "Nevertheless Connecticut Governor Trumbull refuses responsibility for your aggressions on Lake Champlain and the Continental Congress has determined that the forts were attacked in a spontaneous uprising of the neighborhood. Expect an order to restore the Crown's property to its rightful owner, and regard the cannon as borrowed, to be returned when harmony is reestablished between Britain and her offspring."

How is a man to act with such feint-hearted jousters?

June 10, 1775
Crown Point

Easton is back. "At this very moment," says Warner, "he's in secret conference with Colonel Allen."

"Here?" Warner nods and I shout, "Illegal!"

At once I call a council of officers ordering the conspirators to attend, though my authority is the only pressing business. After several minutes, I receive their regrets; "but we are engaged in important business."

I compose a note: "At present I am the legal commanding officer and cannot suffer any illegal councils or meetings as they encourage mutiny. Nor can I tolerate dispute over this command but will give it up willingly to anyone appearing with proper authority."

June 11, 1775

While below, Oswald discovered Allen's scheme to capture both Montreal and Quebec but doesn't know whether it was submitted to Connecticut or the Congress. Allen and his Boys have marched off, I know not where.

June 12, 1775

I headquarter on the *Enterprise,* anchored amid a flotilla of bateaux. From the deck on this sun-filled morning, I was enjoying the sounds of hammering and buzzing on the fortress walls, sign of the solid organization that has been established. One of the guards on duty was Owens, a lad who is grateful that I paid for a doctor when his belly swoll. I saw Easton approach with sagging breeches and stockings. He was weighted with pistols and a sword hanger.

"Password?" Owens asked. Easton pushed my lad aside.

"He's doing his duty" I shouted, "Give him the password, if you know it."

"What password? A fig on your password."

Leaping ashore, I took the liberty of breaking his head; and on his refusing to draw like a gentleman — he having a hanger by his side and pistols in his pocket — I kicked him heartily and ordered him from the Point. My lads cheered.

June 13, 1775

The Continental Congress itself orders the Fort Ti armament taken to the extreme end of Lake George and there inventoried.

My response is the audacious proposal I have formulated in discussions with Oswald to take possession of Montreal and Quebec. I am positive two thousand men might easily effect it.

June 15, 1775

Allen is captured. Defying Congress and Connecticut, the dumbbrave giant directed his Boys to a sudden attack at Montreal. Cornered, he led his captors quite a jig, eluding them by feinting and dodging behind an Indian he had grabbed as a shield. He was paraded through Montreal in chains and is on his way to London as an American curiosity.

June 22, 1775

Colonel Benjamin Hinman is the answer to my proposal. He has arrived with a thousand mud-stained troops and a paper asserting command in the name of Governor Trumbull of Connecticut. "The dervish whirls on," I say in greeting.

Hinman displays his commission and I display mine.

"Your Connecticut commission does not supersede that of Massachusetts." I am most severe, "Until you can show a regular order to the contrary, I retain command."

His gracious, soft-spoken soul is perplexed. "A regular order from whom?"

Now I am befuddled. "From the Continental Congress of the United Colonies...I suppose."

Upon this mild soldier's retreat to Ticonderoga, I sent word that his troops not be allowed in and out of the garrison unless they agree to obey Massachusetts orders.

June 29, 1775

Congress has now sent up a committee headed by Walter Spooner, a snuff-sniffing politican with a sour face and bulging stomach. Brusquely I'm told that my commission is inferior to Colonel Hinman's and therefore he is in command.

"I'll be second to no person whatsoever!"

Spooner runs on like a set of gears, "We are directed to determine whether you should be continued as a Colonel of a Massachusetts regiment or should be discharged. You would do well, Sir, to lay before us your receipts and disbursements."

Intolerable! I order Spooner off my vessel.

July 1, 1775

After two days of ignoring their efforts to confer, I wrote the Spooner committee, "Since you so cavalierly rescind my commission, the regiment I have personally raised must also be rescinded. I cannot, however, release the men until they are paid. Nor can I be summarily dismissed without the return of the sums laid out on their behalf." I listed as best I could the hundreds of pounds spent from my own pocket on necessary supplies.

I delivered this note in person. Spooner responded, "The committee has no such authority."

"But you've got the money."

"Apply to Congress."

And there it stands. The grumbling swells.

July 5, 1775

Spooner has announced that Congress now empowers him to pay those who can stand muster, which means those still capable of fighting. Those reduced by sickness and hard labor are not fit for service and must lose their time.

I collect my sick and feeble and trudge to Spooner's quarters. He emerges, arrogance a bit shaken.

"Are these men to beg bread until they find a way home?"

Nervously Spooner draws out his box, takes a pinch, places it upon his sleeve, and sniffs. After a moment of silent glaring, he turns about and shuts his door.

July 6, 1775

Word flies that I am delivering my boats to the British. Mortified, I burst into Spooner's quarters. "If my enfeebled soldiers are so insignificant that you can toss them away unpaid and disgraced, then by God, I will do what your rotten rumors assert. I'll take my sloop back where I captured it."

This afternoon Easton tried to assume command; my lads clapped him up within a rim of their muskets. I am accused of mutiny.

July 7, 1775

Invited to dine with my officers aboard the *Liberty*, I am clapped up too and confined to a cabin. "To prevent your interfering," I'm told. They bear me no ill will, but believe the kidnappings will squeeze enough pay out of the Spooner Committee to let them go home to their families with honor.

July 8, 1775

The mutiny succeeds where my civility has failed. Spooner's committee agrees to "exceed instructions," as he says. Whatever the physical condition of my lads, they are receiving their back pay.

And me? My outlays for outfitting and supplying the lads? "Apply to the Congress," Spooner insists.

July 9, 1775

Two months ago, I had advanced triumphantly up Lake Champlain. Now as I prepare to descend, holding dejection at bay, a message arrives announcing that General George Washington has appointed General Philip Schuyler Commander of a "Northern Department." That means the invasion of Canada and proper authority, a most welcome gust on a windless day, balm to my bruises.

I quickly gather gear and set sail for Schuyler's mansion in Albany to report on the state and situation of his "Northern Department."

July 11, 1775
The Pastures, Albany

This grand estate rolls for thousands of fertile acres, guarding its Paladin treasure that sits on a gentle rise. The patroon greeted me in the huge entranceway, wearing the new blue and buff of the continental army. Suddenly my lobsterback tunic was gaudy, even though I'd cut the lace from the cuffs. Self-consciously, I explained, "My tailor is accustomed to making redcoats."

Schuyler is large and round with a bulbous nose separating small bluish eyes. His face seems red and grey at intervals. His very movement assumes that deference should be paid. His Dutch family has been rooted in this rich valley for generations.

Inferiority consumes me. I know Spooner has sent a report to him. Does Schuyler think me foolhearty? Surely he knows of my retreat at St. Johns which was otherwise. If he's heard the scurrility cast abroad by Easton and Brown, perhaps he's also heard of my determination to protect mothers and children from the ravages of Allen's Mountain Boys? Does he judge my behavior that of a regular officer? Or is he disturbed that I kicked Easton from the Point and disbanded my lads when removed from command?

But Schuyler was obsessed with the usurper of the New Hampshire grants. As we sat for supper at an oak table set with old silver that shone under a train of French tapers, he asked, "What is your opinion of Allen's claim to New York land?"

I attempted a pose of sagacity, fingers together before my lips. "Frankly, sir, Allen is an outlaw." I realized as I spoke, that I had become rather fond of the mountaineer's brashness and honesty, and said so. It was a mistake.

"Nothing is fine about that rascal. A prince of plunder."

We paused for prayer before the dishes were uncovered. I was grateful for the moment's respite. Schuyler's calm and deliberate demeanor offered me a lesson. Leadership is not seized stridently, not with bluffing, forced obedience, or derring do. General Schuyler's leadership is quiet, inspired by his confident manner. This is the proper, aristocratic mode. The meal was also a lesson. Only the silver and crockery were extravagant. Inside a tureen decorated with enameled animals of the hunt was a simple dish of thick yellow pea soup. Chunks of sausage floated in it. General Schuyler helped himself to a coarse piece of black bread, and using his thumb, covered it with a thick layer of butter.

I did the same, pleased that patroons like Schuyler could indulge mundane tastes and whims. Soup was followed by simple beef and not much else, small roasted potatoes and fried cornmeal cakes. When we pushed back from the table, Schuyler turned the conversation to me. "I'm told Arnold knows when to retreat, thinks to save men and guns."

"You speak of my raid on St. Johns?"

Nodding, General Schuyler filled a pipe and lit it. "I've studied your plan for taking Canada. It came to his Excellency and he sent it to me. Have you ever heard of Montressor's map?"

Indeed I had. Most boys intrigued with the French war knew of it. "Up the Kennebec," I said, "through the Maine woods to the St. Lawrence and the portals of Quebec!" Suddenly fired by the prospect, I expanded aloud, "While another force plods the usual water route through Lake Champlain and the Sorel River, we march through the wilderness. Our sudden appearance shocks them utterly."

My inventiveness gratified Schuyler. "Colonel Arnold, if you haven't made too many enemies, you'd be a good choice for my adjutant general."

Without a moment's hesitation, I said, "I'd rather command the force through the wilderness."

"I see." General Schuyler fumbled with his pipe, then his small blue eyes looked directly into me. "In that case, I'm sending you on to his Excellency."

July 12, 1775

Our spirits are dampened. General Schuyler received news that General Warren is dead, killed at Bunker Hill, a hero. He had been my sponsor and advisor. I've decided to ride home by way of Boston and pay tribute, the deep homage I feel.

July 13, 1775

Worse news. Hannah sends an express that Margaret has expired. I imagine her bony face, flushed, then immobile and ashen, and her stringy flesh, cold. Married eight years, I'd consorted with town strumpets and camp wives. Hannah said "Consumption." Poor lady, just thirty. Never did she complain. Had a cough, now and then.

I set out in a sweltering heat that tarnished everything done and the future glories I'd plotted with General Schuyler. The boys were in my mind, without a mother. What could I tell them? What had I done? Jousted with windbags.

Chapter 4

Narrative of Canada and Captivity
1775

Chose a leisurely route to Canada, by way of Philadelphia and Boston, and missed a golden opportunity. The sloop, *Canadian*, sailed directly to Montreal the very day I embarked, carrying the new Governor, Sir Guy Carleton. Weeks of precious association, pff.

Philadelphia much agitated. Leather aprons and shopkeepers in heated discussions with neatly attired men in Quaker hats. Clusters of them on the busy street. I purchased this ledger thinking to compensate for missed opportunity. Governor Carleton might value observations on the state of affairs.

I can record only the turmoil and gesture, not being privy to discussion. So I doodle — the copula and weathervane atop the marketplace, butchers hanging porksides in the stalls, cabinet makers chipping and carving their wooden blocks, weavers spinning stockings at their looms (addressing each other in German). On Dock Street, I sketched the police stables, the tanyards, mounds of bleached whalebone.

Inns and boarding houses are crowded. "Delegates," explained Daniel Mulligan of the Royal Irish Regiment which polices the city, "birds of every feather."

"Why are the unionjacks at half-mast?"

"You fresh from home? Can't see this country's about to blow?" I shrugged. "Flags're low because these devils believe we slaughtered 'em in Boston. But plenty trouble right here."

"Haven't the offending acts been repealed?"

"Not tea."

"Hardly cause for mischief."

Mulligan offered a bunk in his barracks. In the morning, churchbells toll as if the city's on fire. At a coffee house I hear angry mouths threatening to boycott trade. "The King imagines we're 'mohairs,'" trumpets a red-faced man. "Crown fancies it can annihilate two hundred thousand of us with one blow," echos another. "They think our patriots armed with rusty firelocks and broomsticks," from an older man in a powdered wig next to my table, "and our way of life out of humanity's reach." He is dressed in a red velvet coat with gold trim. His face is crinkled and wears a monkeyish frown. A short, spectacled one standing near directs his loud voice to the older man, "On the contrary, Judge Shippen, we insist on appeasement and the repeal of this cruel tax law." Cruel? A mere matter of the pocket!

Daniel Mulligan tells me Judge Shippen is the "author" of Philadelphia's prettiest belles, "one a precocious fourteen year old. Come to Thursday's dance at Smith's City Tavern, if you're interested." My Julia wrote, "Lady Edgworth has obligingly died, and Richard attends Honora who is more attuned to him than his despicable friend." Of course I'm interested, but I must get on.

The blockade forced our sloop to a wharf outside Boston harbor. Luminous green hills spread before me, spotted with villages and an occasional spire. Warned to wear "colored clothing" rather than regimentals, I hiked in, peaceful and contented.

Suddenly I heard the crunching of gravel, then a herd of rabid men thundering towards me. I scrambled out of their way and fell over brush at the roadside. "Ride, Tory, ride!" Their shoulders jiggled a log pole bearing the shape of a man, pitch dripping from the nostrils and ears, yellow eyes blazing from a blackened face. Spots of the hide were stuck with grey and white feathers. Blood on the thighs. "Ride, Tory, ride!" They hurried on.

I stood and brushed my clothes, explaining to a curious crone puffing a pipe that I just arrived and am on the way to find British headquarters.

"You'd best keep that to yourself. Them's the Sons of Liberty that mowed you down," she told me, "and that's the Reverend Bolton they're ariding in his Bishop's coat." The crone made an effort to laugh, sucked too much smoke and coughed instead. She exposed brownish teeth. "For using his pulpit to denounce Colonel Hancock."

"Had he reason?"

"John Hancock gets a shilling ten for every pound o' tea he can smuggle from Amsterdam, so says Reverend Bolton. That's why the Sons dumped English tea into the harbor. To protect Hancock's profits."

"Truly?"

"T 'aint true at all. Bolton's a lying Tory and they're treating him for it."

"Where are they taking him?"

"Atrottin' village to village as the law provides for strolling idiots and lunatics."

I thanked the crone and she pressed close to inform me, "I wouldn't ask just any loon for British quarters. Find Faneuil Hall in the town center; the army's next door."

Always drawn to architecture, I contemplate the simplicity of the wooden churches which occur more frequently as I come into the city. The streets thicken with shops, carts, carriages, and hawkers. I pass a sailor urinating in the gutter.

The army's two-story structures next to Faneuil Hall are built of huge wooden bricks without any apparent design. In the barracks, soldiers play at cards as unconcerned as if they are in London. A general's aide tells me, "This camp might as well be pitched in the Blackheath. We lead devilish lives here." I'm informed that millers refuse to grind corn for the army and no one will trade with them. "They expect we'll hang Sam Adams any minute. Mad enough to take up arms. I say we squash 'em now or we'll lose 'em."

Sunday. I book a stage called the "Flying Machine" for its speed to Albany. There I intend to sail the internal waterway up the North River through Lake Champlain to the Sorel and St. Lawrence.

Taverns and coffee houses are closed. Having hours to kill before the "Flying Machine" is ready, I attend a morning service. In this glistening house of their deity, the clergyman, a long-necked screecher, invokes the good Lord to smash British ships against the rocks and drown her armies. "Oh Lord, if our enemies fight us, let them have fighting enough. And if more British soldiers are on their way hither, send them, oh Lord, to the bottom of the sea."

What relief! The serenity of snowy Canadian fields after the heated lunacy of the lower colonies.

A schooner carried me along the wild shoreline of Lake Champlain and up the Sorel. I sketched the broken walls of Fort Ticonderoga, the battlements of Crown Point gutted by fire, the heights and length of the dreary sod redoubts of St. Johns, the supplies sprawled over the docks of the military depot at Fort Chambly.

Aboard the schooner I kept out the cold by clustering with a black woman, an Indian squaw, and a boy around a stove in a dungeon-like part of the vessel. Now in this lively city, I am rewarded with the civilized chit-chat I crave. My acquaintances thicken and I begin to sort and select those to associate with. Among the English in Montreal I have several morning invitations, and more for tea and supper. With the French I make parties in the country. Occasionally I drive out a lady in my equipage. We dine, dance roundes, toss pancakes, make noise and return — sometimes overturn — almost frostbit.

My sketches portray the curious birds and animals together with landscapes, prospects, and plans of places. I have also painted the *seigneurs* and Indians at the royal festivities sponsored by General Carleton.

One of my subjects has become a patron, a Jewish fur trader who married into the *seigneurs* and consequently is lord of a grand establishment across the river from the fort at St. Johns some twenty miles down the Sorel. I am amused to discover that

Moses Hazen is a poetaster and believer in Rousseau's natural man. A gnomic creature with dense red beard and myopic grey eyes, he recites Teutonic poems and invents verses glorifying the savages.

The spirit of society reigning here and the winter dress we wear banish the idea of cold. Brightness of the weather, in fact, cheers us. It is a heaven of pure blue, and earth of the purest white. Roads track through the country, over enclosures and rivers, etc. They are planted on either side with fir branches to mark them. Numberless carioles, sleighs, etc. drive about. This account should yield some notion of the appearance of this country.

Before the snows came, I was invited to the ceremonies of the Caughnawaga savages. These gentlemen, clad almost as lightly as our grandpapa Adam, were smeared with vermilion, blue, black, etc. from head to foot. They threw themselves into the most awful contortions and represented with the wildest howling the history of war. The "undress" of the ladies is a blanket impregnated with bear grease, worn capuchin fashion.

I draw these Caughnawagas as Hogarth might see them, in orgy, cavorting with abandon while self-conscious French *habitants* look on and British soldiers gape. One brave lying on a table nurses from a jug as another beats a tom-tom and rattles a gourd. Some white traders are dancing with red men in grotesque attitudes while a neglected urchin bawls lustily. Hovering over all, an old lady in nightcap holds a candle which lights her scorning face.

We are to maneuver on sleds thirty miles up the St. Lawrence. The amusement of the day is to go hunting upon snowshoes, which are large rackets tied to one's feet. Savage tutors will show us how to camp Indian fashion by digging pits in the snow and roofing them into huts. Branches of fir shall serve as my mattress. In short, we are to take humanity a peg lower. Such is life in Canada; today silken dalliance, tomorrow a hut in the style of brute creation.

General Carleton has returned my ledger with a note: "Intelligence of a military nature is wanted — rebel intentions, troop strengths, strongholds, numbers of cannon and mortars, shipping, etc. If you wish reassignment as a regimental historian, see Major Preston." My pen has been hibernating with the bears. Ice on the great river is cracking, the woods awaken. I continue this narrative undaunted, for its own value.

The thaw brings Moses Hazen to town with electrifying news: Colonel Benedict Arnold, a former horse trader in Montreal, is raiding St. Johns. We are ordered out, 475 of us with bugles, flutes and drums, joined by 90 *habitants*, 20 Royal Highlanders, and Captain John Marr, Carleton's engineer with instructions to renovate the fort. A contingent of Caughnawagas leads the procession.

Our drums beat as Fort St. Johns came into view. In the field ahead I saw what appeared dark lumps among the early weeds. It was whispered man to man, "Green Mountain Boys." They rose and groped like actors who have lost their cues. Some still slept in the field. I helped set up the artillery pieces, six of them, while others unwrapped oily rags from their muskets. Then at a signal, grapeshot and musket balls ripped the air. The lumps came alive, comically scurrying in the drifting smoke and smell of burnt powder. Straggling to the boats that brought them, they paddled furiously down the river.

My first taste of hot war. Everything unfolded as in a comedy at Drury Lane. Three captured Boys admit to sleeping off a drinking bout in the field.

As Spring wears in, I sketch the constructions of Captain John Marr and his carpenters, wishing my pen could capture the cacophony of their hammers and saws. I've drawn several sketches of the palisades rising between the redoubts, and the new moat dug on three sides of the fort. From a knoll where I sit beneath an oak, I draw the fourth side, the Sorel, a half mile wide with the fields and woods of Moses Hazen across the way. A few Indians loll about, awed by three dimensional art. Occasionally a bronze hand reaches over my shoulder to touch and smear the sketch.

Scouts report General Montgomery ten miles north of us. He's a British renegade, encamped with 800 New York and Connecticut troops among the mosquitoes on the *Ile aux Noir.*

Suddenly our fort is inundated with frightened wives and children who have been living in huts outside. Neither bedding nor straw can be offered.

Conditions have worsened. Montgomery occupies the road to *La Prairie,* cutting our line of supply, and his scouting parties fire from bushes on the opposite shore, occasionally hitting our bateaux in the river. Major Preston has ordered all the cattle brought in from neighboring farms. Their moo is maddening.

A detachment sent to dislodge the rebels at *La Prairie* has run out of ammunition. I am selected among twenty men to bring up more.

How to describe it?

The terrain like nothing imagined in my military fantasies. Rain soaked the woods. My face was cut from brush; mud sucked my boots. When we emerged from the wild forest onto a field of soaked goldenrod, I stepped on a dead soldier. Blood clotted his hair, trickled down his face and neck. His shocked eyes stared through. I saw four others, maybe five, blood still oozing. For the mud I could hardly tell the American from the British. As I bent to help, someone called, "Leave them, they're gone." We proceeded to deliver our ammunition.

A little cannonade greeted our return. It started when a sentry triggered his piece. Believing they were under attack, the whole fort rushed to the ramparts, firing at random. Later, a dead horse was found in the field, the apparent cause and only casualty of the sentry's alarm.

A fierce wind tore an American bateaux from its mooring across the river; it washed ashore bearing a frightened rebel boy. Interrogating him, we learn of a new American weapon, a mortar called "old sow." It can lob thirteen-inch shells, the boy brags. I think the whole scene a ploy, but am jittery nevertheless. The boy talks also about an army of 1000 marching under Colonel Arnold through the Kennebec wilds to surprise Quebec.

"Tripe!" Major Preston shouts. "No white man's army ever penetrated that wilderness. This pup's a conjurer." He presses the boy, "I suppose you're going to tell us Arnold's dragging cannon and supplies through that jungle?" Obviously it's a hoax, but to what end?

The Caughnawagas in camp heard the same story from an Abinaki name Aneas, who claimed that Arnold sent him to suppliers in Quebec. "Aneas betrayed the American general to Carleton," says a Caughnawaga, "as Abinakis will do."

"Tripe!" Preston repeats.

But the idea of such an audacious march quickens my blood, like ventures in old Teutonic poems. I look across the river to the house of Moses Hazen on the rise, wanting to share my enthusiasm for the heroic, even if the hero is an American. Hazen's field is a howling swamp, framed by hemlocks and firs.

"'Old Sow' brings her pigs to market," observes a barracks wit. It is the 24th day of the siege.

The huge shells take erratic flights, exploding in the water. Before corrections are made, their mighty mortar bursts. Even the Americans are heard laughing. Not for long. This evening the thirteen-inch shells reduced the barracks and houses to rubbish. They blew off the legs of a French volunteer and the arm of a carpenter.

But a simple cannonball created the panic. A barrel of powder was hit, splattering the blood of a Royal Highland emigrant and a sentry. Women and children ran screaming through the gate into a white fog hanging on the river. They trampled and clubbed each other to reach the bateaux. When these were swamped, they attacked fishing boats, fighting the fishermen's oars for berths. Eventually the fog lifted and they crept back two and three at a time like exhausted sheep.

They crowd in cellars of the ruined barracks, out of the wind and cold, while I pace the ramparts above them, fighting the stinging air. Even the wind cannot dissipate the noxious odor from the crush of humanity below.

Morning. A British regular appears out of the woods carrying a white flag. Immediately behind him is a file of rebel soldiers, muskets at the ready. Stiffly the officer tells Preston, "I am here to inform you that Fort Chambly has surrendered and to request permission for our bateaux to pass your fort with prisoners and baggage on the way to internment." Hardly a muscle moves in the officer's face. I feel his embarrassment. Major Preston is astonished. He pulls from the reticent officer the information that Major Stopford, Chambly's commander, has surrendered to a handful of rebel officers after a mere two days of siege. "And not a man lost?" Preston asks repeatedly as though to shame him. "What of stores? You had mountains of ammunition!"

The chagrined officer nods, then asks permission to return three women to the fort. "They wish to be with their husbands when the garrison surrenders."

I watch the bateaux float by, each under a single rebel guard in mudded and torn uniform. By contrast the captives appear fresh in their red jackets. They glide past with their wives and children going to whatever hell of a prison General Montgomery has designated. The sight is like something staged or painted.

Ammunition has become so scarce we were firing only small balls when the ultimatum arrived. It was carried by a swarthy *habitant* dressed in skins from head to feet and led by a rebel drummer across the field before our gates. He announced, "I am Lacoste, hairdresser of Montreal."

Lacoste assured Preston that we had indeed been defeated. General Montgomery's message read, "Should you obstinately persist in a defense which cannot avail you, I will deem myself innocent of the melancholy consequences."

Gauging the messenger, Preston said, "I have heard of a hairdresser in Montreal, Lacoste, who is subject to fits of insanity."

"To assure you I am in right mind and that no relief is possible," responded the hairdresser, "I am requested to guide one of you through the lines where you can see for yourself. When your observer is returned, you can surrender with full confidence that nothing is left but to frame the articles for the garrison."

Amid much discussion, I volunteered, conjuring entanglements on a Byzantine scale as I had fantasized about my father's ventures in the Levant.

Blindfolded and tethered to Lacoste, I followed the rebel drummer. We stumbled through the woods for what seemed hours, every sound exciting me. At last I heard water and felt myself swaying on wooden planks. We were boarding a boat. When the blindfold was removed, I was in a little cabin, staring at a miserable Canadian grandee who protested, "The *habitants* have been unfaithful to the church, to me, and to all the *seigneurs* who fight with Governor Carleton. We are few. Carleton is defeated but has yet to discover it. There is little possibility he can raise another army in Canada."

Suffocating in despair, I choked, "The British shall send him one."

We march through a wet wind two miles to an encampment above St. Johns. Our conquerors receive us with a heady air. I think of triumphant Caesar and the annoying voice in his ear, "Remember you are mortal."

General Montgomery, a tall man with a bulge, stands at rigid attention in immaculate blue. Behind him the rebel lines slouch in their tattered uniforms tied about with rawhide thongs. At a command from Major Preston we halt and turn to face our threadbare captors. Then one by one, we lay our muskets and swords at the renegade general's feet.

Captive! Oh Ignominy! But our "yenkee" captors salute us. ("Yenkee" is the result of Indians originally attempting the word "English," corrupted since to "Yankee.") The rebels respect our military bearing and regal demeanor. They address us with much politeness: "Sir this and that, and by your leave, Sir." This may be mockery, but we are the benefactors. One rebel general is a blacksmith by trade, another is a tanner. I've heard a hatter called major, and common butchers, cobblers and tavernkeeps addressed as captain. All pretend to be gentlemen.

Under guard, our troops go below to whatever place Congress might provide; we officers are ordered to Pennsylvania on parole. General Schuyler, whose guest I am at this moment in Albany, assures me our enlisted men and officers will eventually be rejoined.

Schuyler has traveled in Britain and delights in repaying the courtesies he received. Commander of the rabble, he lives in a mansion here and has the carriage of a royal Dutchman, also the face, an ugly bulbous nose backed by small bluish eyes. His manners exude authority. I have difficulty realizing that such a proper gentleman leads an illiterate, ill-clad mob against officers of the Crown. It would seem General Schuyler could easily be persuaded to rectify his mistake.

Coming down Lake George to my present comfort in Albany, I encountered a blizzard and had difficulty finding a bed. Inns were clogged. It was already dark when I succeeded in appealing to the keeper of a chinky log tavern. He held up his lantern and pointed to a dark corner. "That fat fellow near the window, see him? You skinny enough to fit under his blanket?" I gave the innkeeper two shillings and gratefully picked a way between the forms tossing restlessly on the floor.

"Can't sleep for the howling wind," said the fat stranger. He welcomed someone to chat with. I quickly removed my surtout and uniform, then snuggled under his blanket. We chatted the night. He had been a bookseller in Boston who renounced trade for arms. "I too have renounced trade, and read voraciously." We must have discussed fifty books.

In the morning I watched my night's partner dress. His thighs distended his breeches to the splitting point, I was not surprised to see him cover his belly and chest, shaped like a hogshead, with the blue and buff tunic of the American army. But he was astonished to see me assume the regimentals of a British regular.

"I am Lieutenant John Andre, enroute to my place of parole in Lancaster, Pennsylvania."

"And I, Sir, am Colonel Henry Knox, on my way to retrieve cannon captured at Ticonderoga and investigate the farce perpetrated there by Ethan Allen and Benedict Arnold."

The name, Arnold, gave me something of a start.

General Schuyler claims that Colonel Arnold is the most formidable enemy the British will ever encounter. The rumor of his march through the wild land to surprise Quebec is indeed true. "One of Homer's bragging heroes," says Schuyler, "an Achilles whose act equals his boast."

Blackened cellar holes mark the warpath taken by Pontiac's rampaging tribe through the hamlet of Lancaster some years back. But now Conestogas carrying homesteaders crowd the streets. Lancaster is the threshold to the Ohio country. I am witness to a continent in transition. Rough in dress and language, toting sticks of furniture and Bibles, these hardy families share little with their rebellious countrymen. Perhaps they flee the trash and noise of demagoguery and hope to establish their own quieter world in the wilderness. They pay me little attention.

It was the townsmen who cast the contemptuous scowls as I trudged up a street of taverns to a crude dwelling called Sawbuck house, where I signed my parole. I pledged to keep within six miles of my chosen residence, approach no seaport, nor hold correspondence concerning American affairs. As a prisoner, I am to be clothed by the Crown, but fed and lodged by the Continental Congress.

My gloom lifts somewhat upon learning that all prisoners in Lancaster are under the care of the Honorable Edward Shippen, president of the local committee of safety and father of Judge Shippen of Philadelphia. Having this knowledge, I notice my jailer frowns in the same monkeyish way. He is also addressed as judge, and like his son is faultlessly tailored. "The men of the 7th Foot arrived some days back," he informs me.

I took a billet at the Bird-in-Hand with another prisoner, John Despard, a veteran of fifteen years in the 7th Foot. He is a model soldier who had the regimental standard shot from his grasp. We've become fast friends, acquiring fowling pieces and dogs and devoting our days to upland game, which we donate to the tavern mess. In the evenings we read and reread what books we have or make music. (Despard blows a horn.) On the streets, however, I feel despised. Those who do not avoid my searching glances, return them with searing stares.

Despard is a grumbling man. He threatens to cut the liver from his abusers, and complains the tavern is too expensive. "Are we expected to pay for this hovel with the two paper dollars Congress doles us?" We seek private lodgings. When approached, they spit at us.

Something of a democrat, Despard moans about the misery of the enlisted men in the barracks, half bare in the cold. He is much moved by the hunger of their families who share their rations. Rather than surrender to Despard's moroseness, I try to charm our adversaries and raise a few quid at the same time. Judge Shippen approves my plan to offer drawing lessons. "This town's worlds away from polite society."

I've won over a few of the German settlers by displaying my fluency with their language. One, Eberhart Michael, can answer my flute with his violin. Together with Despard's horn, we serenade the tavern. But not even Eberhart Michael offers private lodgings.

Judge Shippen invites me to a meeting of the Juliana Library Company of Lancaster, "A branch of the American Philosophical Society," he boasts. "You will see the colonies can match the mother in culture as well as battle."

At the meeting I met Mr. William Henry, maker of the deadly Pennsylvania rifle. "The accuracy and quickness of this weapon will end warfare as you know it, Lieutenant Andre." He also displayed a model steam engine he constructed on principles learned from James Watt while in Scotland. Then Judge Shippen performed electric experiments with his Leydon jar and magnets.

"Would you believe a boy can be suspended horizontally by only rubbing a glass tube at his feet?" His demonstration failed, however.

I met the Reverend Thomas Barton. The judge introduced him as "a Tory botanist who defies our more strident patriots by preaching loyalty to Parliament." Barton's son, Benjamin, has become my first pupil. He is joined by a friend, Robert Fulton, who brings along a Quaker boy, John Cope.

Returning from a lesson this evening, I found Despard on the street amid our belongings. "The tavernkeeps are revolting," he scoffed. "They've learned the Congress won't reimburse them."

"How much do we owe?"

"Bartgis claims six pounds. But I wouldn't pay now, even if we had the money."

"The scoundrel must be taught civil manners and respect for British officers."

A silent crowd gathered, among them one of my aspiring little artists, John Cope, who urged his father to take us in. The grim and curious crowd followed as we lugged our belongings to a modest Quaker house on Lime Street. I feared Despard's temper would come loose and lead to cudgeling, perhaps jail.

The tavernkeepers revolt has turned the people's pique to hatred and the aura of it affects our benefactor. This mild but unyielding Quaker is suspected of Troy leanings. Only a few years before, Caleb Cope served as burgess of the borough.

Caleb's family provides its own respite from the scowls and mumblings in the street. They play marbles and hoops on the rug, and the older children join the parents in cards. I devote myself to John's talent, thinking to implant in the bosom of this new world child traditional beauties of the old, while an occasional mob gathers outside and jeers.

We are stoned, windows smashed, everyone but Caleb Cope terrified. The stoning reinforces his Quaker forbearance.

Guiding John's brush, I ignore his grubby nails and note the sensuous fingers. As I lean over to examine his work, the child's feline movement sends a shiver through me. The vacuum in my soul soaks in every feature of my bright disciple, the mobile lips, bisquity odor, porcelain flesh. Honora sans honeyed hair. I shudder at the poisonous notion within. It insults my intelligence, shames me. I share civilization's loathing for such passion.

With steely resolve I continue the drawing lessons, urging the boy to practice the rules, to shade gradually, not blacken the darkest at once but to wash it over repeatedly and never till the paper is dry, to limn the flowing lines of his models, every limb of the tree, and to compare results with originals.

The town's hatred expands like released gas as our comforts are observed. Caleb hears rumors that rebel militia are on the march to string up the royal officers who strut in their redcoats and eat meat while they can hardly get bread. I pay more attention to another rumor, one that has Colonel Arnold negotiating to exchange us for 500 of his troops who have been captured at a place called The Cedars near Montreal. Bizarre but appropriate that Arnold be my inadvertent deliverer.

I project an image of myself free again in England, within the cathedral close at Lichfield, my Julia's grace banishing all shameful passion. The close expands to an endless field of grass grown tall and blown by a hot wind. Running through with extended arms, I embrace all. No restrictions, no censure. These lay in the shadows outside the close.

Thinking it possible, I venture the suggestion that my young disciple come with me, whenever I should return to the mother country. I would take responsibility for the boy's artistic and moral education.

"You are yet a prisoner in Lancaster," Caleb responds, but he does not refuse. Rather he entertains the idea of his son as an adored artist among celebrities of the old country. The Americans abruptly stopped these contemplations. They determined to move the officers of the 7th Foot into the hinterland where "opportunities to do mischief would correspond with their inclinations." Despard and I go by stage wagon forty miles further west to the frontier town of Carlisle.

Distance does not dampen my despicable desire, but reinforces my resolve to eliminate it. Convinced my intentions are pure, I wrote Caleb Cope: "If you decide to let John come, I believe Despard and I can make up a bed for him. A little assiduity and friendship is all I ask of my young disciple in return for my good will, my services, and my wishes to improve the talent nature has lent him. I shall give all attention to his morals. Despard and I are much engaged in playing duets."

Our lodging is a stone house where a mess is shared with eight officers who dress in hunting shirts and trousers like the inhabitants. The hostess is a Scots woman whose fierce black eyes roll between lofty eyebrows and acres of crimson cheek. Her highest entertainment is to observe and question lodgers. She is anxious that our British devotion not corrupt the weak-minded and ignorant. But unlike other Whigs, she seeks no pretext to jail us, for then who would entertain her?

She is not ignorant. "What's good enough for the Roman senate," she says, "is good enough for us, *Your Excellency*," and quotes in Latin, *"Seatus populus que Romanus,* means the Senate and people of Rome."

"I know what it means," I say.

My manner grates on her even more than Despard's. I think she secretly admires him, recognizing in his obstinance something of her own, while she takes my urbanity as effete, my refinement as artificial.

"Trouble is you're a dog at heart, panting to serve your tyrant King."

"You find the rebels different? Is General Washington not called 'His Excellency?'"

"If I had the King of England here, what a pleasure it would be to cut open his body, tear out his heart, fry it over coals, and eat it."

As I was finishing a letter to mother, Mrs. Ramsey called my attention to a scene out the window. Despard was in conversation with two men. "Friends of the Crown!" she declared. Taking my letter for approval before posting, I noted Mrs. Ramsey still positioned at the window.

I stopped to chat with Despard and the men. One, going to Lancaster, offered to post my letter from there. Looking back, I saw Mrs. Ramsey had gone from the window. I gave the man the letter, but before we dispersed he froze on the spot. At the end of the street, a posse of ruffians were running towards us. The two men took to their heels while Despard and I made for Mrs. Ramsey's, regaining the house just as she did. She was out of breath.

This evening the sergeant of the posse demanded to see me. He is a big blunt man, "Thanks to Mrs. Ramsey," he said, "Your Tory friends are in jail. Got almost to South Mountain before we catched 'em." A letter was found on one of them. "Coded, with your name on it."

When the letter was produced, I could not conceal my mirth. I allowed the coxcomb sergeant to stew in his certainty, then calmly announced, "This letter is to my mother, in French." But no one could be found to read that language, not even Mrs. Ramsey who pretends to know Latin. The sergeant has placed Despard and me under house arrest.

Until my word can be authenticated, we read books in our chamber. If we surrender our hunting pieces and appear in uniform, we shall be allowed the streets again. Despard smashed his fowling piece on the fireplace stones. "No yankee rebel's going to burn powder in this gun." I did the same.

For her vigilance, I rewarded Mrs. Ramsey with the coolest disdain. Passing in the hallway, my chin lifted and my head turned to the wall. Upon her entrance to the parlor, I left it. This frozen posture melted the night a Captain Thompson knocked on Mrs. Ramsey's door. Having been her boarder at one time, he was invited in, but declined, pointing to the company of militia behind him. "We marched forty miles to fetch two lobsterbacks."

"What you scheming to do with 'em?"

"Woman, you're obstructing the duty of the Pennsylvania militia."

Mrs. Ramsey would not budge from the doorway. She harangued until the militia hero was forced either to strike her down or give up. At length he departed, shouting to the lodgers crouching behind her, "You can thank my old mistress for your goddamned lives." Sheepishly we brought Mrs. Ramsey a box of perfumed candles, which she refused.

On the streets, ugly with hideous forges and shops, angry hunters brush against an occasional gentleman. They carry weapons transmuted in Lancaster workshops from German fowling pieces to twisted rifles. We are pelted and reviled. Once I was invited to smell a menacing hatchet and told the day would not pass before it split my skull. Another time, a secretive man, Tory no doubt, was kind enough to warn me of assassins waiting to waylay me; he indicated an alternate path. Despard was fired on.

Rumors of exchange are again rife — rank for rank until the supply is exhausted. I prepared a letter for the Copes and concealed it in a drawer. I thanked them and wished to be remembered, especially by John, "Desire him, if you please, to commit my name and friendship to his memory."

The time is come! Orders to move out at midnight. But which way? Towards the British lines or further into the wilderness?

Color appears on the horizon, and our column breaks with frenzy! East! We are marching East. Huzzas till our throats ache. I remember the letter left in my drawer and rejoice in the secret that I am delivered from the snare of John Cope.

Chapter 5

Journal of the Wilderness March
1775

For the Edification of His Excellency,
General George Washington:
Sir: General Schuyler has much improved my original. He proposes a force of 2000 to combat the 500 British Regulars among the annoying *habitants* guarding Quebec. Half to follow General Montgomery through the expected route — Lake Champlain and the Sorel River to the St. Lawrence — the rest to march with me through the Maine wilderness to appear suddenly on the bluffs opposite the city.

We shall follow the path Montressor mapped during the French and Indian war. A few missionaries have used it with canoes, but never an encumbered army. I've made one alteration. Where Montressor followed the huge horseshoe bend of the Kennebec, we'll cut across the ends of the horseshoe, twelve miles straight to the Dead River. Then we climb to the Height of Land where the roaring Chaudiere begins, and float down to the St. Lawrence, materializing before the gates of Quebec.

September 10, 1775
Cambridge
We must hurry to be on the St. Lawrence before the snow. I've sent an express to Rueben Colburn ordering two hundred bateaux to be constructed and on the Kennebec by the time we reach Fort Western. Oak ribs and pine boards for the sides and flat bottoms. He has two weeks.

Messages also to Dennis Getshell and Sam Berry, trappers who deal with Colburn. I want them to scout the trail and arrange provisions. I ask the trappers about Natanis. He's an Abenaki who has been chief of the Norridgewock tribe. Louis, the Caughnawaga chief, warns that Natanis is in the pay of the British. I've also sent word to a few traders in Montreal, asking about inclinations of the mob who attacked the King's statue. They scrawled "German George" over it with mud and put a rosary of rotten potatoes around the neck. I flatter myself that my recent sally at St. Johns inspired them.

September 11

Word has spread over the Yard and I have my pick of recruits. I hope to find woodsmen experienced with white water and robust enough to carry the clumsy bateaux over rough terrain.

General Gates is curious. Pokes into everything, our provisions, guns, even the powder barrels. He pretends to be an earnest advisor. This evening, however, in the dining room at Vassel house, he passed a peculiar remark, "Washington is Arnold's friend." But which of us does he disparage? Does he imagine the gossip of my troubles with Brown and Easton taints his Excellency?

September 14

In three days Eleazer Oswald has raised 1100 men! Still I am not allowed to commission him. "Too many prejudices," which means that Brown and Easton have too much influence. Oswald will be my private secretary and receive private pay.

A merchant with the curious name Return Jonathan Meigs leads one division. He appears devoted to wife and family. Nat Greene's cousin, Christopher, leads another. His major is a blacksmith, Bigalow, whose name describes him. Our quartermaster is a veteran of the French and Indian war, Roger Enos, about fifty and timid, but we need his experience. A Dane, Christian Febiger, is our engineer. Our captains and lieutenants are the best of the lot. Henry Dearborn is giving up medical studies to march along, followed by a snappy hound at his heals. Simon Thayer is just a wig maker but I'll wager a brave one. Our doctor is Isaac Senter, just twenty-two; the chaplain is Sam Spring, recommended by John Adams, "A person with strong convictions and the enthusiasm of a bigot."

September 18, 1775

We parade in the Cambridge Commons before marching to the transports at Newburyport, many in buff and scarlet, cockades and shoulder strips denoting rank, but most in homespun hunting shirts. Captain Morgan wears a leather jerkin with coon-tailed cap, whooping his turkey call.

Aaron Burr and Matt Ogden have introduced themselves with a letter from John Hancock commending them as gentlemen of reputation. Their neat uniforms bear witness.

September 21, 1775
Newburyport

I am greeted with rumors from my rift at Crown Point. "Men won't get paid!" I had to find hard money before they would board. No sooner were we underway, drums, fifes, colors and weeping sweethearts, than one drunk pilot stove his transport on a bar. Now a storm has come up, pelting and scattering our eleven sail, all coasters and fishboats. Some are grounded on mudbanks. Two appear lost in the Sheepscot river.

September 24, 1775
Colburn's Landing

The air is heavy with the smell of pine shavings, but the bateaux are bad, small, gaps between the boards. I have no choice but to order twenty more, stock up, and move on.

September 27, 1775
Fort Western

Messages. One from General Montgomery. He has captured St. Johns and is at Nut Island, closing in on Montreal:

"Having difficulty. The men are impudent with backtalk and bent on plunder." The other message is from Getchell and Berry. They have reached the Height of Land but have not yet climbed it. The carrying places are negotiable, the river shoal on account of the dry season. I've sent out a party under Captain Steele to join them.

Dan Morgan has volunteered to follow Steele and cut a road for us through the great carrying place. Actually he didn't volunteer until I corrected a mistake. I should not have placed him under Christopher Greene. He puffed up. His Virginians understood they were to serve under their own officers. "I accept the authority of no man over my rifles," a position I can appreciate. He has grown a bristling beard, wears leggins and moccasins and a belt clothe like an Indian. His thighs are cut by brush, matching the lash marks on his back. As a wagoner for the British he had been promised 500 strokes but received only 499. "Still owe me one," says Morgan.

An Abenaki claims the Norridgewock chief, Natanis, has seen us and a horde wait at the boiling mouth of the Chaudiere. Also, Mohawks are creeping through the wilderness, thirsting for our blood.

Greene's division starts out today. Meigs will go tomorrow. I am staggering them to avoid congestion at the falls and rapids. Colonel Enos will be last with the provisions.

October 5, 1775
Showhegan Falls

The river narrows and bends so sharply, the water slams us against the granite walls. We've decided to carry the bateaux on poles alongside the tiers of rock and the boiling waters, then come back for munitions and kegs of beef and such.

Lads lay exhausted above the falls, their shirts torn to bandage flesh bloodied by the rock. The rain is already cold. I hate to order them, but we must move on.

October 6, 1775
Norridgewock

Morgan's men suffer dysentery. But they've already patched some bateaux with birchbark and are poling up the river. Morgan urges them on so he can mark the path through the twelve-mile carry.

Waiting for the other divisions, I poke about the deserted Indian village. Natanis is supposed to live here. No sign of him. Abbe Sebastian Rale, the murdered French missionary, is said to be buried in the churchyard. I find the ruins but no grave. That was seventy-five years back, still I feel sorry for the priest. This is a harsh place for a man of any sentiment. I've made a cross of the hard hatchmatac that grows here and stuck it into a nice roll of earth where Father Rale should have been buried.

October 7, 1775

Greene and Meigs have come up and we are counting our losses, a good deal of flour and all the biscuits and salted beef. We must ration the remainder, a square of pork for breakfast and supper, and flour for five cakes a day. But the lads still cheer when I paddle by. One who fell into a mudhole came up with a mouthful. They yelled, "How's the room and board down there?" I laughed stupid and loud as any.

I am pleased to record that my scouts find no enemy activity. Eneas, recommended as a faithful Abenaki, carries my request for supplies and information to Jean Mercier, a trading friend in Quebec. We will cross the great carrying place before he returns, climb the Height of Land and descend the Chaudiere.

We are building a little hospital here. Dr. Senter instructs three aides who will stay with the sick. If the rain doesn't stop by tomorrow, we'll move out anyway. Some are already overeating their rations.

The trees are grey and brown and everything underfoot a shade of mud. But the river is dense with chub and trout. The bateaux float high. Lads pull them along with rope, their bellies full of fish, grumbling about the cold and damp.

When the rain stopped, someone looked up and shouted, "Sugarloaf." The overcast is broken; a flat mountaintop appears between the pressing clouds and patches of clear sky.

October 10, 1775
Great Carrying Place

We follow the path of trees and snagged bushes blazed by Morgan's tomahawks. At a narrow place in the dead forest, our lads filed across a stream on a log. One fell in. It is reported to me that no one helped, so intent were they all on getting across and unwilling to sacrifice their places in line. We've lost the pitiable wretch. But these are decent lads, momentarily out of mind. Each fears to be left behind in the wilderness. Now they are scattered about the fires, dry and rested, bellies full, comrades.

A few who drank the yellow water have become swollen. We've built a brush hut for the invalids. Two lads have volunteered to help them back to our little hospital in Norridgewock. The ailment, they insist, is rheumatism.

October 16, 1775
Portage to the Dead River

Private Henry's seat is patched with birchbark. The scout reports that Captain Steele and his advanced party reached the Chaudiere but would be chewing their moccasins instead if they had not found a map tied to a stake in a stream. It was a drawing of the waterways across the Height of Land. They had taken a westerly instead of a northerly. How the map mysteriously appeared to assist them is a miracle for religious speculation.

Henry is an eager Pennsylvanian, nineteen, perhaps less, bright eyes, a face still cheeky. Food, he assures me, is the key to crossing the Height. Waters are barren and the last animal they shot was a diver duck, which they agreed to boil in the camp kettle together with each man's piece of pork. The broth and pork served for that night's supper and the duck was divided for the morning's breakfast.

Our young private thinks me, and therefore you, Sir, in error. He claims Natanis has been observing us since our bateaux poled off Colburn's landing, but is not a British spy. On the contrary, the Norridgewock have hated the British since 1728, when they shot the French missionary, Abbe Sebastien Rale, who lived among them twenty-six years. Most of us understood from Chief Louis that it was the Norridgewocks who killed Father Rale. From whence young Henry gets his information I do not know. He is a student of law.

Natanis, he suspects, is moved by our hearty lads hacking through the wilderness and his bones tell him it is the Norridgewock chief who left the map for them. I have rescinded the order to shoot Natanis on sight.

We snake alongside the fork-peaked mountain. By turns my canoe points east, west, and south as much as north. The Dead uncoils at last into a northerly course, leaving the forked peak behind. We've been near a month in the wilderness and are collecting ourselves.

Colonel Greene's division is first to arrive, barrels empty. Two wives among them share their husband's rations. I have written Colonel Enos to send up supplies and to send back all those not able to proceed. It may be the means of saving the whole detachment and executing our plans.

October 21, 1775

Still waiting for Enos' provisions. "A windier nor a rainier day I never see," says Sergeant Grier's wife, her skirts held waist high. All gander but none dare a disrespectful word. The sky has turned the blackest blue and the wind screams like a tortured creature. Hemlocks split and crash. Torrents of rain.

October 22, 1775

The morning offers a disagreeable prospect. A lake surrounds us. Small trees bend with the current. Eddies circle around brush and fallen tree branches adorned with bateaux boards, tent canvas, barrel staves, chunks of pork. Morgan's rifles camp on a rise eight feet above the river; Greene's encampment is even higher. Meigs division had to be rescued by surviving bateaux. All are melancholy. But we are not so low we cannot endure worse. Melancholy my arse!

I've sent Major Bigalow with thirty-one men and twelve bateaux to meet Enos and bring up such provisions as can be spared. This will lighten the rear and they will be able to make greater dispatch. I wrote Enos that I have no doubt they will hurry as fast as possible.

October 23, 1775

We find the journey longer than Montressor's estimate of 290 miles. He must have meant a straight line from the mouth of the Kennebec to the St. Lawrence. Before us, unknown wilds, perhaps an ambush by British soldiers and their Indians. Provisions scant. Munitions low, much powder soaked. Rheumatism and dysentery increasing. Near 100 men already lost. And every night now, frost edging the water, coats freezing rigid. Our thrashings in the woods have driven the game off and fish hover at the bottom of the flooded streams.

"To go on," I tell my council of war, "is to race against hunger; to go back is to search for Colonel Enos' commissary. I do not propose running home because my stomach groans. I'm for going on."

Captain Dearborn's thick black beard parts, "To Quebec!" Colonel Meigs echoes, "If I have to eat my breeches getting there." And so the council decides.

What I foresee I did not say in the council, that actual starvation if not far off. The prospect is more terrifying because of this direful howling wilderness. Your Excellency may possibly think us tardy on our march. But when you consider the quality of our bateaux and the quantities of provisions we have forced up against rapid streams (the men becoming amphibious animals they are so much immersed) you will compare our progress with scriptural marvels.

Colonel Greene volunteers to go in search of Enos and Bigalow. He'll return the sick and lame and bring up fifteen days of provisions, enough to get us to Canada. All faint hearts are free to go back with him, better now than before the wall of Quebec. Forty woodsmen are selected to make a dash with me for the settlements. Canoes only. We'll find cattle and drive them back with casks of rum and flour.

October 25, 1775
Height of Land

The snow came as we climbed towards the Height, which is protected by ragged spurs. They are like monster's teeth set to bite any fool daring to invade the Northland. Water flows or tumbles about us, pond to pond, fingers, ovals, hourglasses, some so small we don't bother to break portage but march on, ankle deep. Flakes thicken and the shallow ponds become slush.

We camp before a tooth of the monster, a granite precipice. Montressor's map shows the Height with small, dull peaks. I sketched in my own impression, then slept poorly, thinking of my lads. Their load has already been lightened with so many ruined barrels. Still no company should carry more than one bateaux. Morgan will insist on being an exception. Let him have what bateaux he pleases. Perhaps he'll carry for others. His riflemen steal enough flour and meat to be generous.

This morning, snow in our gear, melting in our wet clothes. We climb the ridges through trees dwarfed and twisted by a perpetual wind, nearly bare sticks gnarled in the prevailing direction. Underfoot, blown-down pine tangled in brush, new growth struggling through, crippled and distorted. Dams of wet debris. Some sink to their armpits in mud holes. As we climb, the flakes give way to icy pins, pricking our faces with the speed of the wind. We stumble through to the foot of the next steep and gaze up, wondering what more must be suffered to reach the summit. Then forward again, catching at every frozen twig and shrub, feet suddenly flying out. In an instant, the wind quiets, the sleet stops. We've topped the Height. A meadow lays before us, a thick green mat, moss needled with ice. Far off where the land falls again, I see a stream flowing north, downhill, as the waters we just left ran south, against us. We are jubilant.

October 26, 1775
On the Chaudiere

The Seven-Mile-Stream, as Montressor marked it, turns into an enormous swamp with twisted alders standing in icy scum as if squashed by a gigantic hammer. I was wading chest high in a quagmire when Captain Hanchet paddled by to rescue me.

Getchell found a finger of the swamp that narrows into a stream and leads us to a shoulder of land around the dismal water. "May be the only way to Lake Megentic," he yells. And I, "We want the Chaudiere!" "Another name for the headwaters."

I order Captain Hanchet to make camp, then select nine others to accompany me on a trial run. Captain Hanchet is upset. I am forced to discipline him on the spot.

We float and carry four miles and ascend to a plateau profuse with alder. Naked roots cover the forest floor. Getchell and Berry lead us down a narrow trail, mysteriously fresh. For miles we tumble over the sharp roots, alder twigs snapping in our faces, until we hear the rush of white water.

It boils over spines of rock as far as the eye sees. We lash our baggage and provisions in the canoes. Getchell and Berry go first, one with paddle in hand, the other with pole to fend boulders. Within minutes, they are stove in pieces. I try. The rapid water shoots me on like a galloping horse. I am a boy again, flying high astride the waterwheel on the Mystic, under and up to the top of the world and around again. Then my poleman pitches over. The canoe careens, strikes granite, rips, and collapses.

Emerging from the icy water, I let everyone know the rest of the army will come down from the Height by foot. I sent word back to jettison all bateaux not needed to carry supplies.

Montressor's map shows the first settlement, Sartigan, sixty or seventy miles down the Chaudiere, which wriggles like a tadpole tail. Bluffs are marked on both sides. The river runs from the bluffs, then runs towards them.

October 28, 1775

Trudging through swamp again, stumbling over dead cypress and hemlock, falling into mud holes. It will be many days this way. My army could starve. I must impose upon the Chaudiere. Use its swiftness...

...I was writing beside a huge fire on a mound of dry land, the men beside me turning one side then the other to the flame. They were discussing hot brown beans in juicy pork sauce when a sucking noise came from the swamp. Everyone scooted for his musket. A large Indian emerged.

He wore breeches and a hunting jacket of fresh leather, and carried a pouch. His face was also like leather. "Abenaki," he announced with composure. The voice was high-pitched. In English he asked for Colonel Benedict Arnold, and handed me his pouch: a message from Colonel Greene:

> I have taken by force from Colonel Enos several barrels of salted beef, pork and flour, slightly damp. All other provisions, medicines, and 400 men are gone. Enos departed October 23, frightened by our sick drifting into his camp with stories of famine, great snows and whole divisions turning back. He believes also that Mohawks await us in ambush on the Chaudiere. I am moving ahead with the main force.
> Lt. Colonel Christopher Greene.

"No one has reported Mohawks," I shouted at the Abenaki. "I told Enos to send back his sick and lame, not his whole army!"

The Abenaki remained still, his small sorry eyes staring at mine as I stared at his. Neither hangdog like most nor puffed with pride like many chiefs I've met. His stillness concealed something. "What are you called? Are your Abenakis in the bush?" I describe these details, Sir, for your greater comprehension.

When my barrage ended, the Abenaki responded, "Your men cross the Height."

I brought forth a Portugese coin and two dollar notes. "What is ahead? Mohawks? British?"

"In Montreal and Quebec."

"Not in the settlements?"

I took his nod to mean no and held out the money. "If our men do not get provisions at once, they starve. Can you help?"

Again he nodded. I took it to mean yes. He refused the money.

October 29, 1775

The Abenaki led us to a place on the Chaudiere where the water merely rolled without breaking. In his feminine voice he informed me that he had fought with the French and would still. He offered a word of advise, "Stumbling increases toward the end of a long journey. The water boils again. But floating is easy the last ten miles to Sartigan." I brushed aside his shamanic pretense.

Within fifteen miles we encountered rapids once more. Suddenly the lead canoe whirled and smashed against the granite wall, another splintered on a rock. I forced mine to capsize rather than lose it.

Carrying along the bank, we descended rapidly, almost running down. Boulders stood between us and the water. When we reached the river again and looked back, the water was far above, falling in green sheets over a great cataract. The Abenaki had not mentioned it. Were I more devout, your Excellency, I'd swear our canoe wrecks were kind impositions of providence. Otherwise all would be dashed to pieces. Around the fire, we damned the Abenaki, his cunning treachery.

November 1, 1775
Sartigan

We walked in file along the bank, Getchell and Steele ahead. It turned into gravel, then a sandy beach. Suddenly Berry broke the file and bore into the sand. He pulled out a whitish green root, bit into it, then dug again, the others with him now, me too, surrendering to our hunger. Our two guides went on.

It was late afternoon when Lieutenant Church noticed the wisp of smoke in the sky. "Getchell and Steele drying their butts," he said, but our weary legs moved faster. Within the hour a field of grain husks came into view, then wigwams, a neat log cabin, behind it the top of a dome with a small cross, a scattering of thatched roofs. Then cows munching hay between whitewashed cottages.

I expected the *habitants* to cower before this collection of gaunt and ragged ghosts emerging from the river. But their dark faces were fat with joy. "*Les bon Bostonnais son ici,*" they shouted. I passed out the French pamphlets I had prepared, "Come generous citizens, under the standards of liberty, against the forces of tyranny..."

They brought wine and bread from their houses, cheeses, potatoes, meat in profuse amounts. I am told Aneas, my messenger to trader Mercier, announced our imminent arrival upon passing through on his way to General Carleton. Overcoming the initial shock, I wondered if Governor Carleton, like others, might choose not to believe the incredible story of our march through the wilderness, especially from a double-tongued Indian.

Salvaging hope, I engage in the hospitality of our French hosts. They have prepared well; a quart of milk, one shilling; a loaf of bread, one shilling; for a chicken, two shillings. With money in hand, I wave at the cattle. Soon Lieutenant Church accompanied by four *habitants* on horse loaded with bags of meal and cheese, drive the cattle down the banks of the Chaudiere to our starving lads.

November 2, 1775

They straggle in as their feeble limbs permit, ragged, wild-eyed scare-crows. The silent line stretches forty miles along the river. When they first saw the horned cattle their cheers passed weakly down the line. I'm told Dearborn and Thayer, stoic Yankees, wept openly, and Dr. Senter was convinced all were hallucinating. Slaughter stations are established every few miles. You will understand, Sir, I am spending lavishly to supply them.

Every account of our route has deceived me. It is longer and has been attended by a thousand difficulties I never apprehended, but if crowned with success I shall think our pains trifling. If our enemy has not been warned of our coming, which is most doubtful, we'll attack Quebec as soon as the men are assembled on the St. Lawrence. I believe we have 600 from the original 1100, Enos having absconded with so many. The most ravenous of them tear the last bit of colon from the cattle's innards. We've lost them by famine, now I fear gluttony. I have ordered otherwise but have not the heart for reinforcement. To avoid the flux, some eat the meat without bread or salt.

James Warner's wife, Jeminy, has come to me seeking protection. She has lost the ration of her doltish husband and offers to cook if she might thereby earn her keep. I record these extraneous lines as memorial to the integrity of woman and the greed of man. Though coarse in manner, Mrs. Warner appears fresh and rosy, owing to our Canadian hosts. She bears her husband's musket, powder horn and pouch. He was a robust man of twenty-five. "A great eater," she says. He consumed within hours all the beef he could get. "We were commencing to march when someone cried, 'Warner is not here!' Another said, 'He sat under a tree.'" Mrs. Warner begged the company to wait. When she found him two miles back, his belly was distended, and he was delirious. Her solicitations to move having no effect, Mrs. Warner placed all the bread in her possession between his legs with a canteen of water, then rejoined the line. May she prove as good a cook as a wife.

November 4, 1775
Ste Marie

A cold and raw day. Twenty canoes appear on the thin ice of the river with twice as many Abenakis. They congregate in front of the canoes, decked in wampum necklaces, robed in fur, faces painted yellow, black, white, and vermillion. Among them certainly is the messenger from Christopher Greene with the high pitched voice. All stand straight as a mainmast. It is said the painted face masks the warrior so that an unfinished foe cannot avenge himself on any one in particular. But the designs are too intricate. They must daub themselves for the art of it. I call, "Which is Natanis?"

One carrying a bearskin and pipe responds, "I am Sabatis, brother of Natanis."

Frenchified English but not the feminine voice of my messenger. Sabatis indicates we should sit and I lead to a barn near the manor house of *Seigneur* Gabriel Taschereau, which I have taken as headquarters. Six of them enter. Sabatis lays his bear rug. An Abenaki sits on it, motioning for me to join him. The pipe, stuffed with crunched sumac leaves, is lit, passed about, and finally comes to me. "Chief Natanis," I begin, addressing my rug-mate, "What is the point of all this secrecy and mystery?"

My rug-mate looks to one sitting opposite. I smoke a moment and extend the pipe to that one. He smokes a while. At last he says, "We are all children." It is the high-pitched voice of my messenger. "You play, I play. You to kill, me to live."

I assure him the *Bostonnais* have not marched to Canada with hostile intent against Indians or *habitants*, but to pursue the King's army who have killed without provocation many women and children in Boston. "We've come to protect you and the French inhabitants from these foreign invaders."

"They want much for their rum."

I change the tack, "Chief Natanis, I am grateful you have helped my men through the wilderness. We suspect it was you who left the map in the swamp."

"And drove animals into your guns and broke paths."

"But you did not warn us of the great cataract on the Chaudiere. The Caughnawaga chief claims you are a spy. I had orders out to kill you. Will you tell me now if we are friends or not?"

"You hear as you wish. I guide in ways you do not know. Courage has carried you over the Height of Land. You will succeed against your enemy. Then do you stay or go?"

Expecting this question from the *habitants,* I had worked out an answer in the pamphlet I had distributed, "*Bostonnais* are the children of people who have taken up the hatchet against them. Now these same people threaten you. We've come to help you drive these people away. We will then return to our own country."

Natanis was immobile. My rug-mate said, "The story is told many times."

"If you will fight with us, each warrior will get one Portuguese johanne a month, a bounty in dollars, guns and provisions, and the liberty to choose your own leaders."

He was as good an actor as ever I was. Before leaving, Natanis had to play out his role as sorcerer and poet, "When the dark angel soars highest his fall is most certain. When his wings brush the sky then the arrow will pierce his heart."

A worse fate than Icarus who merely got his wings singed for flying too near the sun.

November 5, 1775

The element of surprise may be gone but every moment is still precious. We race against British reinforcements reported to be landing at Halifax. Natanis and his braves have agreed to march with us.

Our remaining 600 are reformed into compact companies. They are covered with warm blanket coats the *habitants* sold us, well fed and rested in whitewashed farm houses. Dr. Senter knocked at the house of a merry woman who provided rum and sweetbreads and danced him a jig.

I write letters on a plank before a glowing iron stove. One to General Montgomery. If he can spare me a regiment, I promise Quebec will fall to us, surprise or no. Other letters to John Halstead, a Whig miller, and William Gregory, a trader, both good at filling their pockets but always willing to extend me credit. I'm asking for flour, beef, powder, and boats. Sabatis is entrusted with these messages.

Major Bigalow, who has just reappeared, reports that Dearborn is so sick he cannot sit the horse that was confiscated for him.

"Confiscated by whom?"

The former blacksmith is blunt if anything. "Me."

I remind him of my promise to these people and of proper military conduct, "Although distinctions of office and rank have disappeared on the march, discipline is yet demanded. My example should serve as my command."

Bigalow does not meet my eye. As if to buy his way out of trouble, he offers, "Major Brown is with General Montgomery and has communication with Captain Hanchet."

I have difficulty controlling my temper. Rather than honor the oaf's cunning implications, I give him fifty dollars. "Pay for Captain Dearborn's horse."

November 7, 1775
St. Henri

Arrived at midnight, knee deep in mud. This morning, Dr. Senter and Chaplain Spring hired horses and were soon mired to their arses.

This afternoon, riding the line of march to hurry the men along, I came upon that amiable Private Henry. He sat on a log at the wayside in the hard blowing snow, so wretched he could not put a foot forward. His tricorn was gone, his hair matted, lips cracked, eyes red, a spectacle to terrorize children. Our commissary, he said, had given him as many pounds of beefsteak as he wished to carry. After a savory meal, he found the afternoon march dull and heavy. His head was feverish to my hand. I rode to a tiny house and found the *habitant* who helped carry Henry to a husk mattress, one of seven in the cabin where the family eats and sleeps. The *habitant* swore the stricken boy would recuperate in his care. I put a continental in Henry's hand and two in the *habitant's*.

November 8, 1775
Approaching the St. Lawrence

We are collecting for our last day's march tomorrow. Meeting again, the lads stare at each other, the officers' uniforms so faded and patched they cannot be distinguished from the homespun of the farm boys. Hardly a hat remains among them, and few are the shoes and boots not stitched with rawhide. However ragged and scarecrow, we are reassembled into companies, an army, for the approach to Pointe Levis on the St. Lawrence.

November 9, 1775
Palisades of Pointe Levis

Only a mile, the breadth of the St. Lawrence, separates us from Wolfe's Cove. Snow and wind are whipping the river. Two British frigates appear as antenna'd insects; their galley oars crawl like legs. The earth on the opposite shore thrusts out a tremendous headland, the town combing over half of it, crowned spires and great roofs of green copper. The mass of stone buildings is contained by a wall that ends in a citadel on a promontory they call Cape Diamond. This is the upper town, extending to the confluence with the St. Charles. To the west, stretching away from the wall is the incline of the Plain of Abraham, which is our object. It was here, General Wolfe defeated Montcalm and met his death. Below, the quays and warehouses of lower town are crammed between the cliff and river. Somewhere in the snowy bushes behind is the steep declivity General Wolfe's army ascended to the Plain.

November 10, 1775

General Montgomery promises to join me at Quebec by the time I am ready. He says Seth Warner is in place opposite Montreal with the New Yorkers and Green Mountain Boys, but there is constant brawling, "These sweepings from New York streets are all generals. Many feign illness by swallowing tobacco juice, hoping I shall invalid them home." General Wooster is also a worry, having ordered a court martial without informing either him or Schuyler. Nor will Wooster's men obey any other superior officer. The old cock. What would Montgomery expect?

He has also to contend with Major Brown, who made trouble over placing a battery. For his Excellency's appreciation,

I copy Montgomery word for word: "Unless Brown prevailed, he hinted mutiny was possible. I was forced to call a council and it seemed Major Brown was in control; even Captain John Lamb of the artillery, admirer of yours, sided with him. Necessity obliged me to yield to the general sense. Were I not afraid public service would suffer, I would not stay an hour at the head of troops I cannot direct. As it turned out, we had finally to shift the battery from Brown's preference to mine. This restoration of respect was due largely to the wisdom of Captain Lamb who saw at last what artillery must do and agreed with my position. But this Brown prowls for mischief."

November 12, 1775

The tempest has howled two days. When it blows out, we shall cross. Meanwhile, in spite of their coughs and rheumatisms, my lads continue to build scaling ladders and search for boats. The British have confiscated or burned nearly everything afloat. Caleb Haskell, our fifer, has discovered a forge and with a party is hammering out spearheads for pikes.

The Abenakis contribute canoes and gossip. Easton has joined Brown at Sorel; they have driven out the Highlanders.

Afternoon, the 12th.

There is a break in the clouds. We hear that Lieutenant Governor Cramahe (I believe the name is Hector) panicked at our appearance on Pointe Levis. He threw open all the gates of the upper city and prepared to beg mercy. But Colonel McLean, just arriving from Sorel with 200 Highlanders, burst into the bishop's chapel where the council met, pushed a clergyman from the pulpit, and announced that all talk of surrender was over. Still, the moment is opportune, if we can be sure the storm has stopped. Our scant fleet numbers thirty-five skiffs, canoes, bateaux, and what not.

November 13, 1775
Wolfe's Cove

We crossed in calm water, under a black sky, our motley fleet ferrying several times between shores. The craft I rode was on its third voyage. A half moon emerged as we passed beneath the hull of a British frigate, lighting the spidery rigging against the sky. I feared even the dripping of water from our muffled oars, but the enemy's watch was apparently asleep. We gained the Quebec shore without incident. Immediately, I stopped all further transport. Some hundred are stranded with most of our ladders at Pointe Levis. Captain Hanchet is in charge of them.

From the river's edge, we hear the sentry on the ramparts, "All's well." Matthew Smith has gone to the wall to reconnoiter. Natanis says the gates are rusty, easy to force, and the guards doze. He thinks they lack the courage even to imagine us passing their frigates and patrols this night.

Morgan wants to storm the wall at once. I am waiting for Smith to return, although I doubt his report will be any more reliable than Natanis'. "What has happened to your brother Sabatis?" I ask Natanis. "Has he taken my messages to the British as Eneas did?"

"The Scot has captured him."

"McLean has captured your brother?"

"Only my Abenaki brother, not my Norridgewock brother."

Natanis is difficult, but he has been misrepresented to the Congress and to you, Sir. In fact, it is not too great a stretch to claim our willful misrepresentation of Indians in general has caused us inestimable damage. When Columbus and the conquistadors came upon the red man, he was amiable, open-armed, at least according to Bishop Bartolome de las Casas, whose tome on the history of Hispañole is for sale on shelves of my book store in New Haven.

The bishop gives a disquieting account of the Spaniard's systematic torture and murder in order to enslave Indians in the fields and mines. In these matters the Spanish imagination is boundless. Almost as loathsome was the Spaniards' way of justifying themselves. In this I find many of us unimproved. Their aim was to Christianize, to save souls for God and King. Spanish greed and arrogance created the infamy of these people. In spite of all this, I find at least Natanis and the Abenakis generous where brooding hatred is deserved. Your Excellency may observe certain parallels with myself and the Congress.

I beg, Sir, you do not be quick with this digression. Be assured I burn with desire to annihilate our enemy who are the true conquistadors of the moment. A fig to those who vilify me.

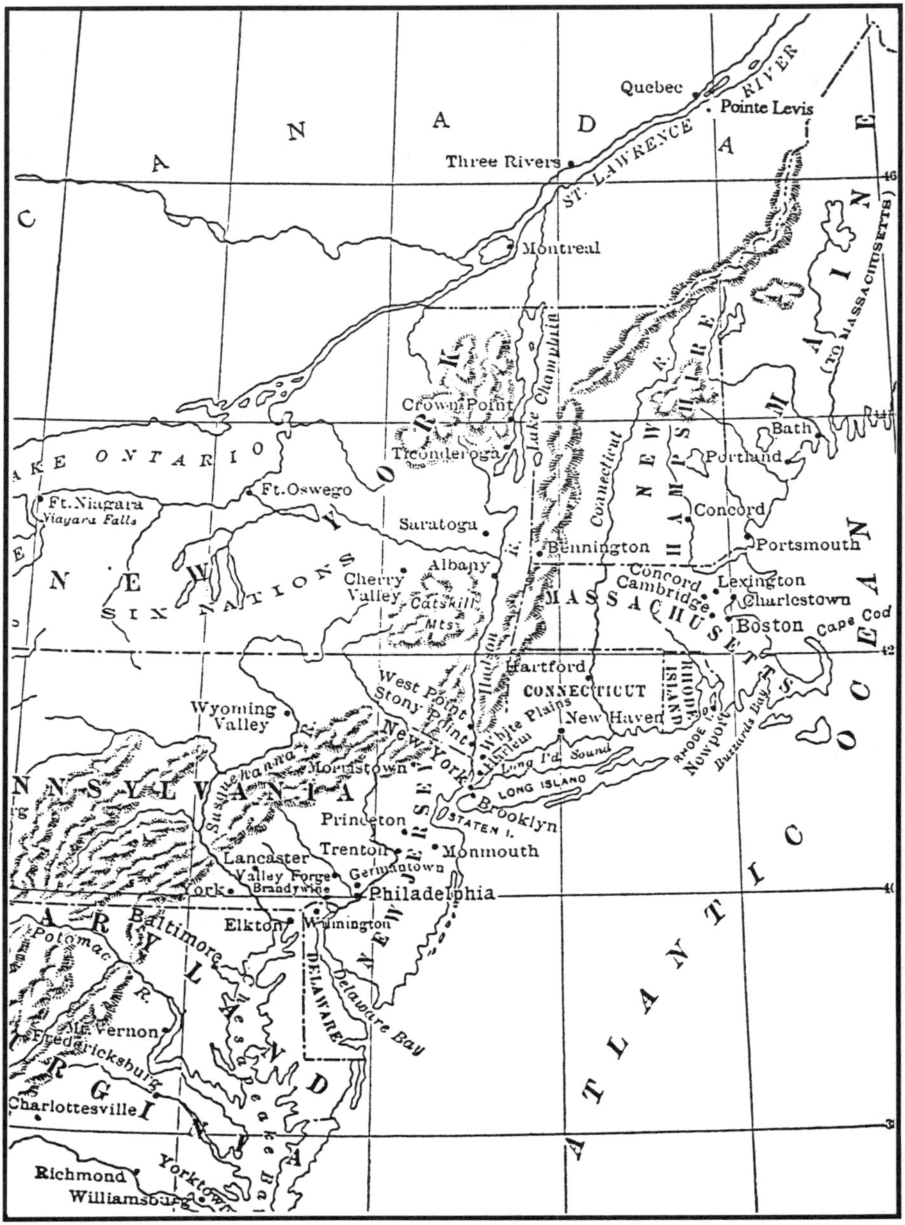
C A N A D A
Quebec
Pointe Levis
Three Rivers
ST. LAWRENCE RIVER
Montreal
Lake Champlain
Crown Point
Ticonderoga
LAKE ONTARIO
Ft. Oswego
Ft. Niagara
Niagara Falls
NEW YORK
SIX NATIONS
Saratoga
Albany
Cherry Valley
Catskill Mts
Bennington
Connecticut R.
NEW HAMPSHIRE
MAINE
(TO MASSACHUSETTS)
Bath
Portland
Concord
Portsmouth
Concord
Cambridge
Lexington
Charlestown
Boston
Cape Cod
MASSACHUSETTS
Hartford
CONNECTICUT
RHODE ISLAND
New Haven
Newport
Buzzards Bay
West Point
Stony Point
White Plains
Harlem
Long I'd. Sound
LONG ISLAND
New York
Brooklyn
STATEN I.
Hudson R.
Wyoming Valley
Susquehanna R.
Morristown
PENNSYLVANIA
Princeton
Trenton
Monmouth
Lancaster
Valley Forge
Germantown
Brandywine
York
Philadelphia
NEW JERSEY
Elkton
Wilmington
DELAWARE
Delaware Bay
Baltimore
MARYLAND
Potomac R.
Mt. Vernon
Fredericksburg
Chesapeake Bay
VIRGINIA
Charlottesville
Richmond
Yorktown
Williamsburg
ATLANTIC OCEAN
46
44
42
40

Chapter 6

Notes on the Siege 1775-1776

Morgan's rifles forced the issue. They found an uninhabited house and against my orders lit a fire. It was to dry out Lieutenant Steele whose canoe had been so overloaded it capsized. Steele threw his arms over the stern of another canoe and was dragged through the numbing water, one man sitting on his clasped hands. I found him at the fire. Dr. Senter was trickling whiskey over his blue lips when we heard the oars of a patrol barge in the cove. I shouted, "Come ashore, come ashore." They backwatered and Morgan's rifles began firing without my order. Screaming came from the barge as it disappeared around the bend. The night's secret is out.

Smith has returned and counsels restraint. The gates are closed, he reports. *Habitants* assured him the British anticipate us, also that Guy Carleton has abandoned Montreal and comes with reinforcements. Morgan is eager to attack and is disappointed in my order to move further from the walled city.

We have found a group of wooden buildings and outhouses belonging to Lt. Colonel Henry Caldwell, who is snug behind the Quebec wall.

Private Henry brings contradictory intelligence. The night we landed, Henry's learned, the St. John's gate was unlocked and guarded by a drowsy watch with a single cannon. Morgan accuses me of allowing these crucial hours to slip by without scaling the wall. No point in reminding him of Matthew Smith's survey. "No more than General Wolfe," I say, "would I risk a slaughter by scaling that wall. You do not know your history. We must entice them out, as Wolfe did, and fight them on the Plain." Morgan insists he knows that history. "So do the British."

We've inherited a herd of nine fat beef and acres of potatoes. The manor house is luxuriously furnished. Hanchet has come over with sixty sick who have the choice of the warm rooms. The rest are comfortable enough in the haymows and sheds. Some find quarters in the homes of French gentlemen.

Still, in spite of the plenty about us, they grumble and criticize my policy of rationing. They clatter for beef and boots. "This policy is a matter of expense," I explain. So they have gone begging. A nunnery and hospital at St. Foye provides them fresh meat and drink. It is on the St. Charles shore, some 50 yards from the school building that Morgan has taken as a guardhouse.

This evening Morgan, Henricks, and Smith awaited me to represent grievances and obtain redress. With Morgan whipped up to the point of striking me, I promised better fare if they guaranteed no plunder.

A picketman has been taken by a patrol on a thrust out of St. John's gate. The captured lad fell asleep and was whisked through the gate before he quite awoke.

Pressed by enemy boldness and needing diversion for the men, I order an advance to some 800 yards of the wall, just beyond the cannon's range. The central purpose is to tempt them out and further to show the townspeople our pride and power. If they choose not to surrender, we can prevent food, fuel, and commerce from going in.

By the time our hatless, patched, and ragged line forms across the plain, the wall is swarming. Through my glass I spot militiamen in green and buff, regulars in red, some kilted Highlanders, and *habitants* in knit capes and belly sashes. They shout as we march and countermarch, never closer than 800 feet. I think I hear "Horse jockey, Horse jockey" in the shouting. To exemplify restraint I find Morgan and stand by him. His face is tight and strained. No doubt he is stressed sorely by the open targets on the wall.

Notes on the Siege 1775-76

Finally I give the signal. Three tumultuous huzzas burst over the plain. The same number of huzzas come from the wall. Laughter follows, both sides. A veritable charivari. Major Febiger takes it upon himself to make a test. He strides forward in clear view and the noise dies. Deliberately he marches until he can see the icy patches in the deep stone trench below the wall. Then defiantly turns about. They wait until he regains our line before unleashing a 36-pounder.

The ball falls short, bounces, and rolls dead. Another follows, then a barrage. We break ranks, waving arms and swearing. Morgan's Virginians dare the King's minions to come down from their ramparts and fight. My lads chase cannon balls and with obscene gestures, display them to the audience on the wall.

Montcalm, the French general, had not accepted such insults to his honor. He marched out to the plain and was thrashed by General Wolfe. Clearly the British would not be so foolish. Again Morgan was right. We withdrew to headquarters, slaughtered a few of Caldwell's cows and feasted.

Caldwell's delicately carved desk provides a properly imperious surface for the letter I compose to Lt. Governor Hector Cramahe. If we are compelled to storm the city, I inform him, every severity can be expected. But if the city takes the wiser course of capitulation, the humanity of General Schuyler will be extended, individuals and their property secured. Three times I send the message with Matthew Ogden under a flag, a drummer at his side; and each time he approaches the gate, musketfire greets him. The Lt. Governor does not deign to employ the civilized rules of war with rebels.

Yesterday, Morgan sent a force across the St. Charles river to search for beef cattle on the east shore, and to observe river traffic at the St. Charles mouth. They saw a ferry mired in the mud. Overloaded with refugees and household stuffs, it was fleeing the anticipated warfare. Morgan's men were helping the crew and passengers push the flat bottom loose when cannon flashed. Balls fell just wide of the struggling passengers. But one took the leg off Sergeant Dixon at the knee. Carried to the house of an English lady, he was given a tetanus and offered tea. "No, madame," he said in pain, "it is the ruin of my country."

Sergeant Dixon succumbed at nine this morning, our first battle casualty. He is buried on the St. Charles meadow with military honors; the men who had hardened to death all along our torturous route to Canada were much moved.

Rumor trickles through the nunnery to Morgan's guard house that the *habitants* are disaffected with their British overlords. On the other hand, a gentleman who hosts our soldiers is disgusted with their rude and ungovernable behavior. He brags that our siege is futile, that Colonel McLean has received reinforcements from Halifax and is devising means to eradicate the annoying *Bostonnais*. He is also of the opinion that the man-of-war *Fell* fought through Major Brown's blockade at Sorel and makes passage to Quebec. It bears Governor Carleton. But Natanis has information that Carleton comes in a canoe disguised as a squaw and takes a turn with the paddle.

Morgan reports two vessels, one unloading men, the other fieldpieces. I order a company by company count of arms and ammunition. Montgomery has taken Montreal. "Carleton," he writes, "has sent up Montreal's defenders and their arms. He departed aboard the brigantine *Gaspe* but was stymied by Major Brown's blockade at Sorel. He escaped by means of a whaleboat disguised as a fisherman in wool cap and blanket coat."

The inventory reveals some 100 rifles and firelocks are damaged beyond repair and too dangerous to fire. Seepage in the kegs has also damaged the cartridges we rolled on the Dead River. Enough remains to issue only five to each man. We are without bayonets.

At the council of war this evening, even Morgan agreed we should not hazard a battle until General Montgomery arrives. I have given the word to march at sunrise twenty miles further from Quebec, to *Pointe aux Trembles*.

Approaching the village by stream, our command craft passed two warships scudding in the current. One was clearly marked with the letters, G-A-S-P-E. The British warships ignored us, hurrying on in the downwind.

I offer to pay the *habitants* in paper (my war chest is near empty). Our hosts may be skeptical but accept anyway in the spirit of the moment. So in many little huts of *Pointe aux Trembles,* hot stoves sizzle with stews of meat, potatoes, and cabbages.

We gather on the church grounds, devouring hunks of meat pulled directly from the pots, guzzling smooth wines, puffing on long-stemmed pipes, pinching their Mimis and Claudettes. And singing obscene yankee doodles in French.

Montgomery's men want to go home before the water freezes solid. "They say they're already slain their dragon in Montreal. Wooster is also troubled. He enjoys quarters at the ancient Chateau de Ramzay while his soldiers take off in such numbers that I fear we'll have neither the spirit nor the strength needed for Quebec."

I remind Montgomery that enlistments are not over until January 1. And that we need, between us, 2000, more or less. And plenty of mortars. I am also asking for flannel shirts, wool stockings, caps and mittens, all his suppliers can provide, as well as rum, ammunition and hard money. The feast was yesterday. Today they spurn my paper.

None too soon we've found a cache of sealskins and are fashioning boots and shoes. The snow rises to our waists and the ice on the St. Lawrence shore bears a man's weight. Rows of pines mark the roads in the snow. Law requires the *seigneurs* to retrace the roads by cariole and horse as soon as the snow stops, whether night or day. Snowshoes are few.

My idle army anticipates General Montgomery. His arrival will reduce me to second in command.

Captain Hanchet refuses my order to transfer some ordnance to Sillery which is closer to Quebec. He claims the water is freezing.

"Then sled on it."
"Too risky."

I threaten arrest. Hanchet has gone off nursing his grievance, whatever it is. I am advised his voice and Lieutenant Burr's are often heard among the grumblers. Eager to replace him, Captains Thayer and Topham toss a coin for the honor. Thayer is loading the artillery aboard three bateaux.

Our lookouts have sighted four ships beating upstream, no doubt to intercept Montgomery. Lieutenant Burr is chosen to warn the general. He is making the most of this assignment, disguising himself as a papist monk or nun, which I find much ado. He carries my introduction to Montgomery as a volunteer and son of the former president of the New Jersey college. "If you need another aide, I gladly offer and recommend to you, Aaron Burr."

The men manage quite well in the weather-beaten houses that cluster on this desolate bank of the St. Lawrence. Their health is restored, sitting in the warm glow of stoves, drinking brandies and wines and frisking with the widows and daughters in unexpected numbers.

At noon, my general arrived aboard a schooner accompanied by two transports bearing the New York companies. His other militiamen have gone home. The New Yorkers appear scrubbed and regular in blue shortcoats with crimson facings. They wear cartridge belts and sheathed bayonets. On every head is a tricorn, the officers with cockades, also silk waistbands and swords.

We greeted the general with an honor guard in the churchyard of the St. Francis de Sales. He inspected them as the first order of business. My hatless lads stood erect in their rags and presented arms as this most soldierly officer with pocked face and tucked-in stomach strode past. In his wake, Captains McPherson and Cheeseman were tall as their superior; and then little Aaron Burr, head up, above the ruffled stock of his new uniform, a captain's cockade in his hat. I worried that one of my honor guards might whinny. Snow has fallen all day.

Notes on the Siege 1775-76

This afternoon Daniel Morgan took the general to Holland House which he has prepared in St. Foye. It is the most elegant of the *seigneur* establishments, wall-papered and decorated with large engravings and maps by the most celebrated artists, inlaid tables, featherbeds, delicately stitched counterpanes, and rose blankets.

As the men unloaded the vessels, stories and rumors spread quickly. Montgomery's father was a baronet on Donegal, a friend of Edmund Burke and Charles Fox. He had forsaken the British army to protest the Stamp Act and married a Livingston of New York, thereupon receiving a recommendation from General Schuyler for appointment to brigadier. But no rumor was so approving of General Montgomery as that of bringing new uniforms. Some of our lads broke into the boxes for verification. They were disappointed.

The unloading of artillery was restricted to John Lamb's company. Squat and tough-looking, Lamb has been an organizer of the New York Sons of Liberty. "Soft, soft," he calls to his men, "You are handling jewels."

Green Mountain Boys are conspicuously absent. But the unctuous Major Brown and the innkeeper, Colonel Easton, are here. At the congratulatory meeting of the armies they stood apart. I'll not describe them.

Though General Montgomery brought no uniforms he assures me he's arranged for them, "Red coats with blue and yellow facings, white woolen breeches, gloves, black wool stockings, fur caps and earflaps. All en route."

"Red coats?"

"Tailored for the British 7th and 26th Foot, who've abruptly departed, ho-ho. Your pretty young men will not be shivering much longer."

He maintained an easy and affable condescension, a grace that forever eludes me. He was minus wig. But his baldness takes nothing from his general's bearing. "I've brought a surprise," he said. "You left Cambridge without bayonets. Though your boys may fear the knife, I'm sure they'll need it."

I asked after the accounts, and was told he would support the expense of all these provisions. I made half-hearted resistance. And he, "We should not consider ourselves indebted to merchants of Montreal who can supply us only with lobsterback tunics." Determined as I am to serve him, I could not resist a contrary opinion, having traded personally with Montreal merchants and being myself a merchant. "Booty!" he responded, "I consider it all booty. What else? Quite as honorable, Colonel Arnold, as the taking of a prize at sea or the running of contraband to avoid the tax." He is at heart a Briton.

General Montgomery also brought intelligence, that Carleton has scraped together nearly 1800 men for the defense of Quebec, including 500 seamen who were mostly victims of press gangs. "They are easily induced to desert," he chuckled. "And we've no cause to worry over Indians. In my opinion he cannot enlist the Mohawks or Senecas or any of the Six Tribe Confederacy because the Crown has tried to make slaves of them."

"Still it is prudent to provide for the worst possible situation."

"Carleton has old men of the Royal Artillery who served Louis of France, eight companies of them, and the militia commanded by an old fool, Lt. Colonel Henry Caldwell, who complains that all should be regulars."

"And McLean's Highlanders," I added, then told him how we enjoyed the comfort of Caldwell's farm.

General Montgomery complimented me on the comfort he was enjoying at the moment. We sat in his corner apartment on upholstered mahogany settees covered in rich figured silk. Outside in the falling snow we heard the cabriolets and sleighs. General Montgomery longed, he told me, for his dear wife Janet.

Putting aside his brandy and leaning to me, he said, "There is rumor below that we've already taken Quebec. And without a man lost. Congress is impatient." Clearly he was anxious to crown his laurels with Quebec, after capturing Chambly, St. Johns, and Montreal. He proposed to deploy his New Yorkers on the plain and my musket companies to the north of them. Morgan's rifles were already in place on the shore of the St. Charles. Then, as I had done, he'd ask for their surrender.

As a messenger, Montgomery had in mind an old woman, Mrs. Baird, who lives in a shack stuck to the side of a cliff but three minutes from the tavern at St. Roche. I suggested our cook, Jemina Warner, who's loyalty cannot be doubted.

I have taken over Morgan's schoolhouse near the nunnery and hospital, while Morgan has crept closer to the wall. His Virginians quarter in a cluster of houses that had evaded Carleton's torch in St. Roche. But they are mostly to be found in the St. Roche tavern, an oak-beamed room with frosted panes. A rumor mill. Gaming tables are upstairs to the rear, open only to *seigneurs* and now to our officers, but it is too cold. Men and officers cluster together around the fireplaces at either end of the tavern room where kettles of stew simmer continuously. Mrs. Baird, a perennial, keeps me informed.

I was upset to learn that Private Henry was among the raiders who sacked Lt. Governor Cramahe's establishment. According to Mrs. Baird, even Cramahe's servants pitched in to load half a dozen cabriolets with mattresses, blankets, silver, and firkins of butter, lard, tallow, beef, and pork.

Responding to my outrage, General Montgomery advised, "The spirit of plunder is the spirit of military aggression. We'll soon have need of it." Disposing of the plunder problem, he went on to something more pressing, "The small pox increases among our troops."

"I encourage the men to innoculate themselves. Dr. Senter reinforces my opinion, but Mrs. Baird insists they are merely scratching in the disease."

"She confuses one pox with another."

"She is convinced that Carleton has sent infected trollops among us."

"What's to be done?"

"I've ordered Dr. Senter to close the hospital to all pox victims and put them into quarantine at Sillery."

General Montgomery nodded his satisfaction.

Mrs. Baird observes that Captain Hanchet is frequently at a tavern table with Major Brown. He treats the men to cognac and harangues them to follow him home when enlistments end on New Year's Day. I have ordered Hanchet to duty with Morgan near the wall. (On the day General Montgomery escaped a ball that killed his sleigh horse.) But once more he refuses.

"Let Hanchet have his rope," Montgomery cautions. "A court martial might result in mutiny." I see now how discipline has troubled the general. He spends too much of himself avoiding problems and dreaming of his Janet's warm bed. Meanwhile the tavern buzzes. Mrs. Baird reports that Hanchet plans to combine the companies and create a new regiment to be commanded by Major Brown, promoted of course to Colonel. She says Brown speaks to them of inalienable rights, their freedom to complain, to select their leaders, and partake in military decisions.

Montgomery tells me that Brown's promotion to Lt. Colonel has been compromised by his plundering the baggage of his prisoners at Sorel. It is the first I'd heard of Brown's pillage. "And he's not publicly impeached?"

"Contain yourself, Colonel. A trial could damage us here in Canada. Its enough he's forfeited promotion."

"He's so informed?"

"Indeed."

It is most painful to reflect that after all we have endured on the Kennebec, the Height of Land, the Chaudiere, we sit now in futility, our singular purpose of surprise sprung awry, and I awaiting my general's pleasure, however I admire him as a gentleman, while my restless soldiers spend their energy in plundering and plotting. What was the point of our impossible march? Except that we have done it? Reward unto itself, like *Pamela's* virtue.

But the point is to take Quebec. My resolve is in no way diminished.

Addendum

My promotion to brigadier was at first denied. I spent six weeks in the *Hopital Generale* (nun's hospital) at St. Foye, my leg a prisoner in a pallet box and that denial in my breast. We were still into the siege when I was removed to the Chateau de Ramzay in Montreal and the good news finally arrived. It was dated January 10.

The packet contained a letter from General Schuyler who explained that Congress had to be shamed into the promotion. He also wrote that Congress at last allowed 819 dollars as the balance due me. The money was sent to Hannah.

But to the siege. I shall quickly conclude these notes.

Montgomery agreed to let Mrs. Warner carry our ultimatum. General Carleton made a show of her. As she handed him the ultimatum, his hand withdrew as from the pox, and it fell to the floor. A servant was ordered to pick it up with tongs and submit it to the fire. They put poor Jemina in the city jail and in a few days we watched as corps of drummers emerged from St. John's gate, rattling and rolling, and made a lane for Mrs. Jemina Warner to march through; the people on the wall jeering and shouting obscenities. Oh she was proud! Looked straight ahead and swung her arms.

Responding to Carleton's insult, we had Lamb set up his artillery behind some houses within range. His tough boys struggled to root their howitzers in the thick ice. But Lamb's "bombettes" just tickled the wall. Carleton's guns then destroyed the houses, exposing Lamb's artillery and blowing it to bits. After that, I went personally with another ultimatum, this one promising Carleton and Cramahe safe conduct to England. I waited over an hour, freezing before the wall, expecting either an opened gate or a cannonball. At last an aide called out as if to an illiterate militiaman, "Tell your general the governor does not treat with traitors." I was advised that Montgomery should implore the King's mercy if he wished any communication.

By now everyone knows what happened next. Our plan had been to attack at night under cover of snow. We believed a sudden assault at an unsuspected place would carry us into the city. While Major Brown made a feint at the St. John's gate, we'd lead our armies around to the lower town, Montgomery clinging to the St. Lawrence while I'd wind through the warehouses and docks along the St. Charles. Montgomery planned to meet at the stone stairs under Cape Diamond, and together we'd ascend to the upper town within the wall. I could not imagine two armies squeezing up a stairway into fire, but Montgomery was my commander. If we got that far I'm sure Carleton would have slaughtered us.

Snow fell on Christmas day and the alert was sent throughout our camp, but Matthew Smith got high as a skunk that day and let it all out. If we hadn't canceled, the outcome might have been otherwise. Next day, the wind shifted and the sun came up. Enlistments ran out December 31. If another snow did not fall before then, we'd have to attack anyway.

A blessed nor'easter blew on that last afternoon of the year. Smith was sprawled on a tavern table, Steele led his company. Our lads put hemlock sprigs in their hats to identify themselves; some wrote "liberty or death" on strips of paper and inserted them with the hemlock, all futile in the blowing snow. It was so stinging, our pickets had to be changed every fifteen minutes. As we marched, the snow became a rush of horizontal pellets, numbing our cheeks and iced brows. It hissed and spit and piled against doorways and barricades. Faces down, the lads held coat lappets over the gunlocks to keep them dry. Some artillerymen let go their ropes and lost their cannon sleds in snowdrifts. My hand, momentarily bare to check my pistols, stuck to the cold metal.

Montgomery was hit some ways from our meeting place. He was rallying his New Yorkers while his carpenters were sawing a passageway through a barricade. When they had enough opening to reveal a blockhouse, cannon shot straight into them, rockets lit the air, and all the bells of Quebec rang out at once. He was calling, "New Yorkers, follow your general and Quebec is ours." McPherson and Cheeseman fell with him. Burr was there too, but disappeared.

The next morning, while Colonel McLean's Highlanders were celebrating their New Year Hogmanay, General Carleton had the bodies dug from the snow. One wore a fur cap with the initials R.M. The right hand held a British sword with ivory handle. They might have called him a traitor, but buried him tenderly with the honors due an English officer.

While in the *Hopital Generale* at St. Foye, I received notice of Montgomery's promotion to Major General and a letter from Janet asking about her husband's watch.

A story runs through the hospital that Morgan made it to the second barricade on the Saut-au-Matelot, that's the narrow passageway through the Palace Gate where I was hit. Morgan refused to give up his sword to a British officer. Tears down his powder-blackened face, he just happened to spot a priest standing about and give him his sword. I'd not vouch for that story. But I do remember the dead hunched against the wall as I was dragged to the hospital; Lamb coming in with his eye and cheek blown away; Steele with a bloody blanket over his missing fingers; word flying through the wards that Carleton was making a sortie into St. Foye with fixed bayonets; and our frightened wretches hobbling between the windows and my cot.

I commanded everyone to load whatever they had and whoever possessed a sword to lay it on the bed beside him. "I intend to kill every Briton who dares enter this hospital!" The nuns were horrified. We waited, it seemed days. Before I went into coma, I heard carts crunching on the snow, alarming everyone, but they were just hauling bodies to the ice house. Carleton chose to stay in his citadel. When they released Meigs, he told me the governor treated his prisoners with humanity.

All the time I was delirious in that hospital, our lads kept the siege, though less than 500 were effectives. Dearborn was so lost among the warehouses in lower town he just stumbled into captivity. Natanis was wounded and let go on the promise he would return to his traps on the Dead river. The men were outnumbered three to one. They slept on their arms in ice forts they built under the Quebec wall. I sent to Wooster in Montreal asking for a competent commander to replace me. He gave me himself.

Dr. Senter says the ball that downed me passed through a few bones and my Achilles tendon. All I can remember is transforming myself into a wild animal, as usual, and whipping my men into a fever. Then blood was oozing from the top of my boot and Parson Spring and Private Henry were helping me to the nun's hospital, about a mile, most of it through fire from the wall. Two lads were shot as they paused at the sight of their immobilized leader. "Rush on, brave boys," I'd shouted weakly, "Rush on!"

Benjamin Franklin

Chapter 7
Reflections on Montreal and Valcour
1776

Brown told Congress that I conspired with Canadians to turn a guinea for myself. Actually we urged them at bayonet point to take our paper for the flour and pork we needed.

What irks my distant relative? Not jealousy alone, that I have just been promoted, but the discovery that I will not recommend his promotion. In honor I cannot until the matter of the prisoner's baggage is resolved. I owe that much to General Montgomery.

After I exchanged commands with Wooster and was healing at the Chateau de Ramzay in Montreal, Brown demanded a court martial to clear his name. The Board of War found his charges groundless.

The *seigneur* in charge at the Chateau was Moses Hazen whose assistant was a cunning oaf, James Wilkinson. Wooster had left the place in great confusion, not one contractor or quartermaster. So I sent to Schuyler for a commissary officer to relieve my burden, thinking also of the hard money Schuyler might send along with the new officer. Instead, I was ordered to appoint Wilkinson. And one day he refused my order to purchase blankets, imagining I would turn them to my own profit. "More mercantile than military?" Wilky sneered.

"And you are more nice than wise," I answered, which he probably took as a kind of confession. I just let it go.

I paid no mind to Hazen either, until stories began circulating that I was consigning goods bought for the army to agents in New York and Albany. Hazen's disloyalty should not have surprised me. He had alerted Carleton when I scouted St. Johns, and the next year, when Montgomery attacked, he'd befriended Schuyler, who commissioned him into service.

I dispatched Hazen to Chambly and got on with the undoing of Wooster's blunders, I had also to put up with the bishop's drivel and infernal ritual. Then I heard that Brown had gained the ear of Dr. Franklin and the old philosopher was coming to find me out.

Dr. Franklin and his Commission.

Officially the Franklin commission came to see if we could establish relations with the *habitants* and Indians. If not, the commission had orders to stop all funds and shut down in Canada. En route to Montreal, Franklin and his commissioners were invited to spend several days at Hazen's great house on the Sorel opposite St. Johns. Being a thinker and reader, Hazen impressed Franklin as Brown did. What he wanted was the commission's support in his fur trade. And he could offer them good relations with the Indians, at least the Caughnawagas.

I imagine the commissioners enjoyed Hazen's hospitality as much as they did mine, but the Congress heard nothing of his reception, only that mine was overly ostentatious. I was acting under orders from General Schuyler. Frenchmen respect a good show. I threw open the Chateau and offered wine to everyone who came to pay respects. And aware of Dr. Franklin's propensities, I gathered a number of ladies for a feast with the best bloods of the parish.

He was tired. The only lady he encouraged was Mrs. Thomas Walker, and that, I believe, was because we quartered him at *L'Assumption,* her house just outside the Montreal wall. Between washes of wine, Dr. Franklin informed me that he had little faith in our mission. "Why would these Catholics not consider Governor Carleton a safer ally than Protestants from Independence Hall?" The logic was irrefutable. I agreed and added praise for Governor Carleton's graciousness. He had returned General Montgomery's watch gratis when Janet was offering to pay any price.

Reflections on Montreal and Valcour 1776

Under the illusion that Franklin had come with bags of hard money, I ventured, "Our lads have not been paid." I had about 11,000 in paper, owed the lads three times as much and the *habitants* some 15,000 hard. The *seigneur* on the other side of Franklin, a mustachio'd voucher-holder with slick hair, was straining his ear. The great man said he brought no specie, only paper. Immediately the *seigneur* jumped to his feet as if to make a toast, but instead cried out *"ai ete vale," I've just been robbed.*

Franklin was also disturbed by first hand accounts that Burgoyne had landed at Halifax with 10,000 fresh troops, mostly Germans. "This conflict," he told me, "is no longer a family quarrel. We must end it, at least the Canadian part."

Still I felt he was testing for my reaction, perhaps for some assertion of enormous will to carry on. But an unfortunate incident reassured him. Hazen had constructed a stockade to protect the Caughnawagas from the St. Francis and Mohawks at a place called the Cedars, which is opposite the tip of Montreal island. It is a strategic point of defense and I had reinforced it with a small garrison. Just before Franklin left, the British came downstream with a force of 160 Indians and attacked the stockade. They captured the entire garrison before I was able to send relief. We hunted for boats to pursue while Louis, the Caughnawaga chief, carried my warning: "If one American life is lost to your savagery, General Arnold will destroy all by fire and sword."

In turn, Chief Louis was told that if Arnold dared follow, their Mohawks would massacre the captives. The Caughnawagas rowed me to the Cedars where the men had just been evacuated. Five were left, still alive, staked to the ground, naked, blood frozen over their wounds. Whatever the consequences, I vowed to destroy my enemy. I sent for Moses Hazen and called a council of war. We argued and insulted one another until I broke up the meeting in disgust. Hazen convinced nearly every officer to oppose me.

I tossed all night. Perhaps I shouldn't have sent for Hazen. But it was his stockade. In truth, I found myself weighing his view. On one hand, we had enough men to satisfy my rage for action; but on the other, I envisioned the sacrifice of those unhappy wretches. Before morning, Chief Louis led two British officers into my tent who asked if I was convinced the Mohawks meant to murder the prisoners. I had to admit I was. If I withdrew and if Congress would release an equal number of British prisoners, they would vouchsafe the return of all our men. It was the answer, heavensent! I submitted, trusting Congress would uphold me.

I should have known what Hazen would do. Once the men were returned, he cursed me to Franklin for selling out my country. Dr. Franklin interviewed a few of the released prisoners; they knew nothing of my arrangement. Mostly, he listened to Hazen, who swore the Mohawk captors treated all with humanity, and whoever said to the contrary was an enemy of peace and fallacious disturber of mankind.

When Dr. Franklin was departing — with John Caroll, another commissioner, and Mrs. Walker, she to join her husband in Albany — the old man asked would I help him satisfy a friend in Congress. Of course I would. Getting into the coach, he grunted and spoke at once, "My friend wishes to know why Major Brown has not been recommended for promotion." When he was seated at last, I told him of the plundering at Chambly, but he already knew. "A number in Congress," he responded, "have suggested if the baggage was plundered, Arnold must have done it. And if I am pressed to explain my opinion that an alliance with these French is impossible, you must know, Colonel" — I was now general — "that I will be compelled to say it is because our high command is robbing the merchants."

Now sooner had Franklin arrived in Philadelphia than a shock wave jolted Congress. They saw my agreement at the Cedars as extortion, which it was, by threat of murder. I was accused of lining my pocket in a secret part of the arrangement. My commanders at the Cedars, Colonel Bedell and Major Butterfield, were drummed out of service, and of course Congress would not honor my word to the British, not until Washington insisted.

Now I was desperate to get out of Canada. One commissioner remained, Sam Chase. He directed me to confiscate everything possible and issue certificates of promise. With Burgoyne's ships on the St. Lawrence only a day's sail off, we boxed all the confiscated goods, marked each parcel with the name of the merchant who owned it, and hurried the bundles to Chambly for storage. Major Scott, in charge of the transport, delivered them to Hazen's wharf as directed. But Hazen was nowhere to be seen. Lame as I was, I galloped off for Chambly. On the wharf I found the boxes torn open, ransacked of the silks, linens, plate, and hardware we packed. The merchants descended upon me, waving their vouchers, *"Votre argent ne vaut rien! Ou est ma marchandise?"* Immediately, I wrote to General Thomas, who had replaced the inept Wooster, "The merchants demand their merchandise. This is not the first or last order Colonel Hazen has disobeyed." Thomas was just about dead of small pox and never read my note. When Hazen returned, he demanded a court martial, charging me with plunder.

At that time, the British had just routed St. Clair and Wayne from the fort they captured at Three Rivers, and a column was marching to the Sorel. I ordered a retreat. But Sullivan, who replaced Thomas, countermanded me. I pleaded with him to quit and secure our country before it was too late. That would be more honorable than hazarding battle against superior forces. General Sullivan was not to be advised by an inferior. So I wrote Horatio Gates, now second to Schuyler, that we had lost in one month all Montgomery was a whole campaign gaining, together with an amazing amount of money. Congress had forsaken us. We were pricked with every want, discipline vanished, soldiers pox-ridden, and a powerful enemy advancing. If we conducted a safe retreat, I wrote, "we could still hope fortune might shine again."

I'd begun my own withdrawal, descending to St. Johns, when Sullivan at last sent the order to retreat. The lads loaded bateaux, then lit up the sky with everything flammable. Jamie Wilkinson and I helped the lame and poxed board the clumsy boats, some carrying others, the remnant of an army. Then we watched them paddle away, past the burning barns and buildings, and Moses Hazen's grand place across the river. I started to enter the last bateaux, but drew back, ordered Jamie to mount, and rode with him towards Chambly for a last look, the smoke from the fires burning our eyes. Within minutes we had to turn about. Through the trees we spotted glints of lobster red, of brass from the light artillery, and of fixed bayonets.

Chief Louis was at the landing. It should have been Natanis. I hardly knew Louis, even maligned him when we first met at Washington's camp in Cambridge. Now as an old friend he came to wish me Godspeed, the only one of all the Canadians. We embraced. Then Jamie and I shot our horses, leaving nothing to the British. I waited for him to enter the bateaux ahead of me.

He claimed later that I indulged my vanity. Being the first to come, I had insisted on being the last to leave.

The Hazen Court Martial

Of course I countercharged. The court was called in the midst of the summer's heat while I was constructing a fleet at Skenesboro, a mosquito-infested shipyard at the southern tip of Lake Champlain. The timing annoyed me. Working with house carpenters, I was frantic to shape the green forest wood into gondolas and galleys before Guy Carleton's great warships pursued us down the lake. Fortunately ten miles of shoals and rapids below St. Johns delayed the British fleet. On July 28, the day the Declaration of Independence was read to us, I learned that Carleton was laboriously disassembling his huge men-of-war and reconstructing them on the other side of the rapids. I hurried to the court at Ticonderoga.

Controversy was rocking the Northern Army. Schuyler, sick for all his seeming vigor, clung to Albany. Gates had been appointed, not second to Schuyler as I thought, but to an autonomous command. Gates, a squat, red-faced butler's son is a popular champion of the people while Schuyler, the patrician, assumes a natural right to rule over the lesser born. Though esteemed the equal of the patrician, Gates shows deference, seeming to accept a subordinate roll. But their relation is uneasy. Looking up to Schuyler, I nevertheless get on with Gates. For a while I served to soothe the fracus.

Gates was convinced I was the proper person to command our fleet. "I have advised General Schuyler," he wrote, "that one who is perfectly skilled in maritime affairs undertakes the command of our fleet upon the lake. Schuyler is relieved of great anxiety. I am convinced you will there add to the brilliant reputation you have so deservedly acquired."

My only difficulty was the fact that General Schuyler had already appointed a commander on the lakes, so claimed a 'Commodore' Jacobus Wyncoop. As with the Allen affair at Ticonderoga, no one informed Wyncoop he was replaced. The 'Commodore' challenged: "I know no order but what is given out by me."

A bit feverish with malaria, I was in no mood to argue. "You surely must be out of your sense. If you do not obey my orders you will be arrested immediately."

He refused; I sent him to General Schuyler under arrest, recommending he not be cashiered if by the time he reached Albany he appeared sorry. But the whole affair worked against me, coming in the midst of the Hazen uproar. A fatality seems to attend every one of my enterprises, a reputation which brands me rash and unreasonable, a brigand in officer's uniform.

As I anticipated, the court at Ticonderoga noted "the disputatious temperament in the cavalier and disrespectful manner General Arnold replaced General Schuyler's appointed commander on Lake Champlain." The court was also cognizant of Major Brown's charges that "General Arnold mistreated and plundered Montreal merchants." General Poor, the court president, refused to hear testimony of my chief witness, Major Scott, who delivered the goods to Chambly. He declared Scott "an interested party."

Seizing the advantage, Hazen claimed the merchandise confiscated at Montreal was never delivered and was not vandalized or plundered by him or his soldiers but stolen by General Benedict Arnold himself, "for his own private gain."

"I am not the one on trial here," I protested.

General Poor refusing to silence Hazen, I erupted, providing evidence of "disputatious temperament." I denounced the proceedings as unprecedented and unjust, whereupon General Poor found the "whole of the general's conduct during the trial marked with contempt and disrespect. His protest is illegal, illiberal, ungentlemanlike. Nothing but an open acknowledgment of his error will be satisfactory."

I flared out of control, "It is you who must apologize to me! It is the court who casts ungenteel and indecent reflections on a superior officer. And however you may think, not one of you is infallible, nor the whole court together. Congress will decide the justice of your decisions. But this I assure you, I shall ever, in public or private, be ready to support my character. As your very nice and delicate honor is injured, I will not withhold from any gentleman of this court the satisfaction he may require."

The court acquitted Moses Hazen with honor. They ordered me arrested.

But Gates intervened: "I am obliged to act dictatorially and dissolve this court the instant it demands General Arnold be put in arrest. The United States must not be deprived of that excellent officer's services in this important moment."

Battle of Valcour Island

At the beginning of August I received intelligence that the British fleet was preparing to continue pursuit down the Sorel. As soon as the wagons from the coast delivered our rigging, I proceeded up the lake with the clerks and farm hands I'd made into sailors. Land cannon were mounted on our crude gunwales.

Gates cautioned that I temper my rashness and, "stay close to the American end of the lake. Be prudent as you are brave. Avoid wanton risk or unnecessary display."

My response was shrill, "I beg that at least one hundred good seamen be sent me immediately. We have a wretched motley crew; my marines are the refuse of every regiment, and few of the seamen were ever on salt water."

For practice we aimed guns but could not waste powder in firing them. My recruits brought news that Washington had been driven from New York. The catastrophe forced a grave new responsibility on our poorly manned and ill equipped little fleet. Suddenly we were the only remaining line of defense.

We anchored in a narrow channel between Valcour Island and the New York shore, my hidden vessels pulled into a half moon.

Down they came, sails billowing before a strong wind — the great man-of-war, *Inflexible,* two schooners, twenty gunboats, four longboats, and twenty-four bateaux loaded with troops. They passed the island bluffs, not spotting us until they were two miles down river. I had in mind to turn up the lake behind them and sail for an attack on St. Johns. That would wipe out their supply line, but the wind was unsuitable. Discovering us, Carleton turned about, and made clumsy tacks into that strong wind.

They crept up to some 350 yards of our half-moon and then the huge guns of the *Inflexible* blasted away, their 12-pounders hitting our *Royal Savage*, which went aground. The narrow channel prevented their tacking and their progress stopped. Sails fluttered, the wind turning them this way and that, while guns thundered. I dashed about the deck of my flag ship, the *Congress,* aiming and firing cannon, one after another, dodging as rigging came crashing down, and cheering on my lads, some beyond my voice in red pools at their guns.

We endured a whole day of it on the choppy water, masts broken, sails shredded, blood running over surgeons' aprons. The *Congress* was hulled a dozen times and received seven shots between wind and water. As the fog came that evening, flames from the beached *Royal Savage* reflected in the lake. The clumsy *Inflexible* caught a gust that moved her into point blank range. We took five of her broadsides before darkness stopped the battle. Sixty men lost, half our fleet sunk or ravaged, and most of our ammunition gone. Even as we huddled in council aboard the *Congress*, a gondola, the *Philadelphia,* was going down. The common opinion was surrender or be wiped out.

Anyone who's seen an evening fog over Lake Champlain would understand what I did next. Their warships blocked our escape and we hadn't enough ammunition to fight them come morning. I remembered the night we slipped an army past the warships guarding Quebec. So I ordered a lantern be placed on the stern of each boat and hooded, to be seen only by the vessel immediately behind, all other light to be extinguished, no oars to be dipped in the water, and no more sail than necessary to move along the bank. Our half moon uncoiled like a snake into a single file, one boat a hundred yards behind another, creeping silently through a black mist under their very noses. We could hear their pumps and their talking. As soon as we were out of range, out came the oars and we hurried towards Crown Point, over twenty-five miles off.

A good wind the next morning was their blessing. It favored their big sails over our slow gondolas. We had hardly any canvas remaining. They caught us passing Split Rock and raked us with cannon and grapeshot. Two of our ships ran ashore, one surrendered. The *Congress* ran with the enemy ships astern and one alongside, firing incessantly for near three hours.

Our sail, rigging, hull, everything was torn and shattered and four men killed, but he returned what he got. When we counted seven sail surrounding us, I ordered my lads to row windward, a direction their canvas could not follow. We dashed up a creek and set our battered vessels on fire, flags still flying.

Through the forest, we kept an eye out for their Indians; two days without sleep before we reached Crown Point. Gates was upset; I had disobeyed his warning to stay at the American end of the lake, and lost my fleet. Publicly he damned me with faint praise, "Few men have met with so many hairsbreadth escapes in so short a time." The commander of Ticonderoga was not so gentle: "Arnold, our evil genius to the north, has got us clear of our fine fleet, after going to the mouth of the enemy contrary to the opinion of all the army."

But I built that fleet. And I spent it wrecking Carleton's warships, by God! He had to withdraw to St. Johns. Begin all over. It gave Washington a whole winter to recoup his fleeing army.

Before the new year wore in, Congress promoted five inferior officers to seniority over me.

Chapter 8

Letter to Anna Seward 1778

Philadelphia
May 23, 1778

My dear Julia,
    I no longer ask why men kill each other. Your Cher Jean has become a soldier. How else shall I begin after so many years?
    I trust Honora drew strength and happiness from Lord Edgeworth before the end. The sorrowful news reached me upon release from captivity and distress shrouded the joy of that event. I am at last able to restore some balance. Do you read this in Honora's "dear blue region" or beneath the shade of Canon Seward's "good green people?" Sweet memories ameliorate the anguish.
    Captivity exposed me to the loathsome side of the American character. Dining as gentlemen in the officer's mess is one thing, but living in daily torment, threatened with your life, spat upon, and humiliated by unwashed rabble is quite another. Their cruelty and obnoxiousness are enough to turn the souls of the most forgiving men. Yet my bitterness does not fester, I am committed to advancement.
    Let me begin, then, with New York, the destiny of our long march after the exchange of prisoners. It is no longer the tranquil city of Dutch traders. Rebel-dug trenches trickle with slush and garbage the Hessians call "spoiled sauerkraut." Foul odors mix with the aromas of Sugar Island spices and coffee coming from the wharfs. The nut trees and water leeches are gone.

Stumps remain, some cut cleanly, others charred from the great fire. The view from Trinity Church down to the river is spiked with stark chimneys standing among the ruins. But on the herringboned brickwalks, gentlemen in wigs and taffeta still stroll with their silk and pastel ladies. And the noises are much the same as I remember: the hagglers before the Merchant exchange, the auctioneers on Coffee House bridge, the longshoremen's groaning chants on the ropewalk.

On the march I kept a journal and mapped the countryside. Sir William Howe, our Commander-in-Chief, was much impressed with the maps and granted me permission to purchase an available Captaincy in the 26th Foot. He also promised a staff appointment should one occur. I spent the winter in Staten Island where the British Crown shone upon gentlemanly and agreeable companions, most notably John Graves Simcoe of the Queen's Rangers.

Simcoe is possessed of a great chest, tart tongue, and monumental scorn for rebels. In the Spring I visited Oyster Bay with him. Aside from hunting small game along the coastline, his interest was in the Townsend girls, particularly Sally, a taunting sweet whom I believed somewhat drawn by my softer approach. My robust comrade put me in mind of Honora's remark that "women are for the enjoyment of the warrior." But Sally confided her opinion (is fratitude my lot?) that Simcoe is actually afraid of her because she is brunette rather than blond. "My body threatens to engulf him in a whirlpool of ecstasy, which endangers his self esteem. Blondes he associates with Britains whose purity he fights to protect. America must be destroyed because it empowers the lascivious brunette." (I relate this delicate item for your private amusement.)

Good as his word, General Howe recommended me as aide-de-campe to General Charles Grey, a 48-year old veteran scarred by numerous wounds. Almost immediately Grey offered his opinion that Howe was a friend to the American cause. "And his brother, the Admiral, is no better. The Howe brothers call the enemy 'misguided children of Britain.' On Long Island General

Howe joked while Washington escaped with 900 troops right under our noses."

It is so, Julia. Howe's dulcinea, Mrs. Loring, wife of his commissioner of prisons, provides all the glory he envisions. He believes the American dispute will evaporate when the child realizes his situation. As for the parent, the less damage we inflict in disciplining the naughty child, the easier to make amends. He would punish, not with vengeance, but loving regret.

Grey, on the other hand, is a professional whose purpose is to thoroughly defeat the enemy. One who shrinks from killing and burning is incompetent, which is not to say he cannot be a jolly fellow. General Grey laughs heartily at my witticisms, deserving or not; yet when necessary he drives everything from mind but war. I have learned to do the same. Even my letters to Mama and my sisters are chilled with military jargon.

Last July we marched onto transports, expecting to sail up the North River in support of Burgoyne's invasion from Canada. We would cut the colonies in two and subdue them piecemeal. (General Clinton was to hold New York with 7000 troops.) But to our utter consternation, we sailed due south! This in spite of Burgoyne's urgent messages to come up the river. Told that Arnold had been rushed to the northern scene, Howe merely responded that the apothecary general would provide comic diversion for Gentleman Johnny's entertainment. Meanwhile we would occupy the rebel capital.

Sailing for the Delaware, we encountered contrary winds and calms. Whole days were lost as we lay motionless, our decks like ovens. Troops collapsed daily, horses perished in their stalls. By the time we reached the Delaware's mouth, the enemy was long forewarned. We encountered strong fortifications on the Chesapeake Bay, but strangely no fire as Admiral Richard Howe guided us with line and plummet through the shallows. The admiral had prepared flat boats on the Elk river. We transferred and pushed upstream. Houses along the shore were empty, barndoors hung open, a few frightened faces peering out. But the land was lush. Foraging yielded quantities of flour, garden produce, sheep and cattle.

We passed through the country in easy stages — picking up the Tory John Galloway whose coach followed in the rear — until we approached the Brandywine river where Mr. Washington waited in force. In an involved rhapsody, he had persuaded his troops that we could be exterminated. He even granted them his own share of our baggage which they could plunder. When General Knyphausen took their cannonade at the river's edge, Washington sent an express to Philadelphia boasting that the Americans had stopped the British army. But Howe and Cornwallis had marched up river with our main force, crossed, and came down hard on the rebel right.

The Americans were astonished when Cornwallis bore down and Knyphausen charged directly into their fire at the same time. But Washington had sense enough to drag his unwilling myrmidons to several commanding heights rising one above the other like an amphitheater. Howe was content to let them run.

We marched towards Germantown, which rims the rebel capital, annoyed only by General Wayne's rifles sniping at our supply wagons in the rear. Our brigade was ordered to get rid of the nuisance. Ulysses could have done no better than General Grey. Setting out on a black night, we searched every house and forced a blacksmith to reveal Wayne's headquarters outside a town named Paoli. Grey now addressed us: "Firing discovers us to these squirrel hunters, not them to us. Surprise and speed are required." He would employ a measure learned in Germany; I was sent from company to company to make sure every man had removed the flint from his Brown Bess, and had attached his steel.

Their fires guided us till we heard their singing and fifing. We stole upon Wayne's pickets. None managed a shot, one escaped. Suddenly the music stopped; shouts of confusion rose. The enemy were silhouetted against the fires, attempting to form files and marching into each other. Drunken soldiers react slowly. We rushed in, slicing throats and crushing heads at will. From my position in the rear, I heard rebels trying to surrender, our men yelling, "No quarter!" Musket butts smashed mouths into silence. Some escaped to the woods, screaming like hyenas. I joined in the search of camp probing for wounded who might be playing dead. Discovered, they implored mercy. But Grey demanded his orders by obeyed. They were skewered or bashed a second time. Our light infantry are the nastiest ruffians in his Majesty's army.

We liberated the gin intended for throats now stilled and continued the party we had interrupted — toasts to his Majesty, General Howe, General Grey, and especially "Mad Anthony Wayne," the American general who was a tanner of cow hides. Grey gained much credit for this coup and is now respected in the army as the "no-flint general."

Howe and Cornwallis led our columns into Germantown, the Tory Galloway still trailing in his coach. Citizens who had been patrolling for rebels now thronged the streets as our grenadiers marched in, singing "God Save the King," while bearded Hessians in brass-fronted helmets caught children's extended hands in theirs.

Now my only danger was being spoiled as a soldier. Evenings I rode out to an elegant country seat called Clivedon, belonging to the exiled chief justice of Pennsylvania, Benjamin Chew. His family, particularly his daughter, remains in residence. But how can I describe Peggy Chew? Most delicately made, slim of waste, fine-boned, pearly face, and deep dark eyes less melancholy than pert. At seventeen, a keen and canny woman.

Thinking the war about over, we were aroused one foggy morning in October by musket fire. General Grey and I jumped into our uniforms, grouped our men and rode through the haze in the direction of the fire. Broken companies came running at us in a state of havoc. We worried the whole regiment might panic into wild retreat. But no pursuing rebels materialized. We were told that a Colonel Musgrave with six British companies had holed up at Clivedon and were rebuffing charge after charge. Encouraged, we rushed up the streets in the thick fog. Scrambling through gardens and orchards, we received fire but did not see our enemy. We heard the drum beat for a parley, which some confused men mistook as the signal of victory, others as the signal of defeat. Both sides joined in the pandemonium. When I thought to withdraw, it was pointed out that the Americans were fleeing. Grey came by shouting to gather troops and follow him.

My horse must have carried me in circles for through the fog and powder smoke I made out once again the stately mansion of Clivedon. The sloping lawn was strewn with a prodigious number of dead. Some decorated the veranda and lay near the windows. The stone was knicked with shot. I realized the firing had stopped and that I had actually flourished a sword. My mount suffered four or five buckshot. Oh that I had received them to make people stare with my story of five wounds in a day! The rebels had fled like rats. I was exuberant. How feeble, after all, are the forces that menace this world.

It had been the glorious victory one dreams, yet the Americans continued raiding our encampments, kidnapping and killing sentries. Then fireworks lit the night sky and deserters told us they were celebrating triumphs in the north, a *feu-de-joie*. The wildest rumors had Burgoyne surrendering. We had no way of knowing until an officer arrived from the quartermaster-general's department. He informed General Howe of an agreement made with the rebel General Gates. Burgoyne's beaten army was returning home, to serve no more during the present war.

May 24.

Grey and I are billeted in agreeable circumstances amid books of Benjamin Franklin, whom John Galloway disdains as "the printer who works with his hands." Dr. Franklin's householder provides candles and other comforts. Our sloops deliver all the West Indian turtle we can digest. Simcoe has acquired a new doxy who drove down the line in an open carriage reviewing the Queen's Rangers. He follows the example of Sir Billy Howe, now snoring abed with Mrs. Loring, while the enemy languishes at Valley Forge.

General Grey has appointed me his intelligencer, a peculiar route to glory. In other capacities I am indispensable. Eager to please, I write bawdy little sketches to celebrate promotions. With sweetness and light I counter those who disdain "no-flint's" butchery at Paoli.

Officers, a committee of three, invite the city's constellation of beauties to weekly balls at Smith's City Tavern. The troops are also entertained at such places as Moore's Alley where cock fights are popular. (Do I embarrass you? Have I not become a soldier? Let me plunge further. Wet nurses are more than ample to supply the demand; comely white bondwomen are escaping servitude.)

We have an exhibition of glowing pictures and a sale of racy books in the marketplace; last week the college offered a lecture on electricity. A dozen churches are in the town, but the rebels have removed their bells. The streets are paved with brick and well lit. Houses are generally furnished with rush-bottomed chairs, pewter platters, wooden trenchers. The finer homes contain silver tankards, China punch bowls, mahogany-framed mirrors and teaboards. I believe the people loyal though professing neutrality. Taking their ease with Madeira, they mutter, "Let who would be king, we know well who will be subject."

Our officers of title have the belles and mamas in constant titillation. Shrewd Peggy Shippen is amused. A warm friendship has sprung up between us, indeed with her whole family. Judge Edward Shippen is among the first men of Philadelphia. He wears silver-and gold-laced coats and has been fined repeatedly for neglecting his military duty. Lord Rawdon, our adjutant general, considers Peggy the handsomest shill in America. All are in love with her. She was the centerpiece of Captain Hammond's glittering dinner aboard his man-of-war *Roebuck*.

I am also under the spell of a Miss Becky Redman whose silhouette I cut from the card of an invitation she extended. Does my Julia conclude that her Jean is adrift or bewitched? And I've not mentioned the rapturous brunette, Becky Franks, whose sensuality sets British bones aquiver. Alas, she's chosen her lord, one Sir Henry Johnson, and will soon journey with him to New York. The voluptuary, Simcoe, bemoans missed opportunity. Becky complains that she's spent few evenings at home since we British arrived. When we reopened the Southwick theatre, even those evening were taken.

In spite of the Quakers and Presbyterians who opposed us, our first bill, *No One's Enemy But His Own* proved so popular, servants were sent at 4 p.m. to hold places. We soon added a professional, Miss Hyde, who sang "Tally Ho" between the play and the farce.

Such was our amusement. It ended abruptly last month with the announcement that Sir Billy is called home. The cause, I suppose, is indolence, especially vexing in the light of Burgoyne's defeat. We have little to show for all the expense of occupying Philadelphia, except for a few forays. (Simcoe's Rangers bring in rebels caught stripping the market people. They are decorated in their spoils — eggs, vegetables, and the like — paraded through the streets, whipped, and drummed out of town.)

One of Sir Billy's last acts was ordaining a lottery to raise 1000 pounds for the city's poor. Whatever his shortcomings, his dissipation and lack of discipline, and however Mrs. Loring taints the army, the troops express great affection for him. I am surprised by this emotion and swept along in it. However dismal his performance afield, I do not believe there is another instance of a Commander-in-Chief having so universally endeared himself. Even General Grey is affected.

That our sentiments might be known, we resolved to give Sir Billy a send-off befitting his character. It was such a pageant as America has never seen. Remember the extravaganza General Burgoyne staged to celebrate Lord Stanley's marriage? He dressed the guests as shepherds and shepherdesses, produced a play for the occasion, and climaxed it with fireworks and a masque. Twenty-two of us subscribed over 3300 pounds to outdo Burgoyne.

Our Mischianza (meaning a variety of entertainments) recalled happier days when knights were unimpeded by commoners and jousted for the favors of their ladies. For the sake of the dancing that followed, we sacrificed the armor and decked ourselves in costumes of the court of Henry IV.

The ladies, one for each of the fourteen knights, were attired in polonaise and gauze as Turkish maidens with sashes

Letter to Anna Seward 1778

spangled according to the colors of their knights. Their turbins were embellished with feathers, tassels, and seductive veils.

Judge Shippen suffered a spell of moral indignation when a group of Quakers called, deploring the licentiousness of our celebration. It was unseemly that his daughters appear in costumes of Turkish strumpets. This was the previous day, the costumes made, paid for, and delivered. The judge, nevertheless, refused to let his daughters partake. They yelled and screamed, Peggy tossing crockery in a tantrum, but Judge Shippen would not yield, not this time. Peggy's eyes were puffed when I picked up the costumes for others to wear. She was most appealing.

The entertainment began with a grand regatta. Wharves and housetops thronged with spectators as we drifted down the Delaware in three galleys to Walnut Grove, the abandoned estate of an exiled Whig. The *Roebuck* hailed General Howe with a seventeen-gun salute as we docked. Spectators massed at the jousting field where the knights' ladies were seated on conspicuous sofas. Spears were shivered in the first encounter, pistols fired in the second and third, swords flourished in the fourth. Ladies were so fair and knights so brave, it would have been impious to decide in either's favor.

Reconciled by happy compromise, the Turkish maidens unpinned favors from their turbines which they presented their knights for prowess. The ball followed, continuing till ten when the windows were opened and a gaudy display of rockets began the fireworks. Supper was announced at midnight. Large folding doors were thrown open, revealing a magnificently lit salon. Blacks in oriental dress with silver collars and bracelets ranged in two lines and bent to the ground as the general approached, his eyes enchanted with the unexpected perspective of ornament and illumination. Four hundred covers were served, twelve hundred dishes.

But an explosion disturbed the night's rapture. Jealous rebels had sneaked to the town's outskirts and lit camp kettles filled with powder which burst like Chinese firecrackers. Instantly, drums were beating the alert. Howe's cavalry rode off in pursuit. With great presence of mind, the general announced,

"The grandest fireworks are saved for the last." More toasts followed and the whole repaired to the ballroom where daylight overtook us in all the festive mirth that animates youth.

Perhaps none of this is news. England, no doubt, has heard and is indignant at such a triumphant celebration given a commander who has all but lost a war. A dragoon, asked to explain the difference between the jousting teams, offered, "The one are tom fools and the other damned fools."

My pen is worn and my well dry, dear Julia. A word from your gracious hand, nothing so prattling as this, would sanction my every undertaking. I blush to recall asking for Honora's postscript.

Adieu and again adieu,
Cher Jean

Chapter 9

Battles of Freeman's Farm

A Memorial by a Participant
1777

My purpose here is to explain my impulsive and impolitic behavior at Freeman's Farm and its contribution to America's greatest victory, incorrectly styled, "Battle of Saratoga." Further, to assign proper credit where due. If I write plainly rather than prettily, pray excuse me in the name of candor.

In that service, I preface this memorial with the sentiment of a broadside sold in my New Haven shop immediately after the battle of Concord Bridge. It also expresses the fate of many a British gallant at Freeman's Farm:

> How brave you went out with muskets all bright
> And thought to befrighten the folks with the sight;
> But when you got there how they powdered your pums,
> And all the way home how they pepper'd your bums,
> And is it not, honies, a comical farce,
> To be proud in the face, and shot in the a-se?

Burgoyne boasted he would promenade through America with an army of 10,000. All he had to do was scatter plunder, and the rebels would be too occupied to fight. He aimed to capture the sleepy Dutch town of Albany and then join Clinton climbing up from New York, thus isolating New England. Already he had alarmed the country with his quick capture of Fort Ticonderoga, spending not a ball of grapeshot. Arthur St. Clair, a subordinate who had been promoted ahead of me, fled when he espied

Burgoyne's cannon atop a commanding hill which he himself should have fortified.

At Fort Edward, I found Schuyler's army demoralized by Burgoyne's easy victory. The fort was dilapidated, ill-supplied, and swarming with refugees fleeing Burgoyne, their carts stuffed with furniture. Only their Bibles and sick children distinguished them from camp followers.

General Schuyler was utterly dispirited. Coughing and clearly ill as we talked — the patroon and the apothecary — he damned the civilians who ruled the new country and criticized his command. He knew Horatio Gates had replaced him in all but title. "If Job were a general in my situation he'd not be so famous for patience." Schuyler was ready to resign rather than submit to further indignities.

Being the gentleman he is, the general worried about me, would I be able to subordinate myself to those promoted over me. I had already discussed the point with General Washington and agreed to swallow pride for the good of the country.

"I'm confident I won't be inferior much longer."

Schuyler fiddled with his pipe, drew a deep breathe, and said, "It appears you are too brazen. Your appeal for restoration of seniority has been denied. The civilians are opposed."

Though he had just himself talked of resigning, General Schuyler pointed to his shortage of general officers and convinced me it was better to continue than return to a grumbling civil life.

I was in camp less than a week when Fort Stanwix sent an urgent call for relief. Stanwix was a stronghold to the west along the Mohawk. It was under siege of Colonel Barry St. Leger leading a wild band of Iroquois. A council of officers argued that Fort Stanwix must defend itself. We could not weaken our position just as Burgoyne was preparing to attack it.

"Where is the brigadier who will command the relief?" Schuyler asked. Silence ensued.

Schuyler lit his clay pipe and sucked it a time. Then he described the affair at Oriskany, where St. Leger's Iroquois massacred a group of volunteer farmers. It was hand to hand, tomahawks and spears against knives and musket butts. "Those who came to bury the fallen found white and red locked in death's grapple, the most brutal butchery of this war." But his voice was weak. He puffed, waited, then added, "If those Indians take Gansevoort's defenders at Fort Stanwix, they'll storm down Mohawk Valley, scalping every woman and child, torching every settlement. When they reach this camp, their frenzy will drive us into Burgoyne's arms." Another pause. "Already, the Iroquois have slaughtered and roasted whole families while very polite and humane British troops looked on."

Still not a brigadier came forward. The silence was unbearable. "I'll take it," I called, and stepped out, the only major general in the room besides Schuyler.

Camp spirits rebounded. When the drum beat for volunteers, nearly a thousand lads desired to be under my command. Going off. I took General Schuyler's instructions with a warm press of the hand.

Encamped several days later at German Flats, I received Schuyler's note, "John Adams has succeeded in his plan to put Horatio Gates at the head of the Northern Army." Nevertheless, Schuyler invited the usurper to Old Saratoga, his summer house, but Gates rudely declined.

I wrote my new commander, "We have offered bounty and recruited all who would swear allegiance to the United States. I leave this place with 1200 continental troops and militia to relieve Colonel Gansevoort. You will hear of my being victorious or no more. As soon as the safety of this part of the country permits, I will fly to your assistance." Rather uppity for an apothecary, but then I was addressing the butler's son.

Luck was with me in the form of Hon Yost Schuyler or Cuyler, a half-witted half-breed vaguely associated with the general's brood. He was clever enough to carry out a hoax I devised, rushing into the enemy camp with the story that the ferocious white chief, Arnold, was descending upon them with as many troops as leaves on the trees. Holes were shot in his coat as proof he had just escaped from our camp. We sent an Indian after him, who arrived out of breath with confirmation, "Arnold is coming!" Believing that half-wits are inspired by God and thus innocent of deception, the Iroquois ran, followed by the soldiers, and finally by St. Leger himself. Boundless joy! My name was sufficient to scatter them in panic, throwing off arms, knapsacks, and blankets as they fled. As Burgoyne captured Fort Ti without a shot, so I saved Fort Stanwix.

Returning, I was ordered to select a site and build fortifications with the Polish engineer, Thaddeues Kosciusko. We decided upon a rise some four miles east of Indian Spring (Saratoga). The height commanded the river road leading to Albany. It bore the name of the innkeeper at the foot, a Mr. Bemis, who was informed that General Gates would take his tavern for headquarters.

While the men were constructing earthworks, I worried that Gates might rely on these fortifications for defense and just wait to be attacked. Such strategy was his military advice to others. As major general, I assumed the customary position of his deputy. It was my duty to question his strategy. But he had been cool since I returned from Fort Stanwix. His only message to me contained no praise for the rout, and the words, "Ever so affectionately yours," had been struck through.

My deputy, Matty Clarkson, was convinced that our *ruse de guerre* at Fort Stanwix had perturbed the commander. "He's jealous of the shouts and cheers you receive while he's greeted with a silent salute and presentation of arms up and down the line." Davy Franks, my other aide, disagreed. "Gates still resents your disobedience at Valcour Island." The commander became absolutely icy after his aide, Henry Brockston Livingston, requested a transfer to my staff. It was no more than the insult to me when my aide in Canada, Jamie Wilkinson, reappeared as Gates' adjutant.

Not until Gates countermanded one of my orders did I confront him. I had assigned newly-arrived militia to brigades; he decided to dispose of them differently and gave a direct counter-order, placing me in a ridiculous light.

Behind a makeshift desk of two tavern tables, Horatio Gates was an unmilitary sight, a fuzzy face of clay with a snout for a nose, stringy wig caked with powder, and a squat, paunched body. Through his glasses, the eyes looked askew, never focusing directly. But Granny, as the men called him, was a trained soldier, respected for that. He was also ambitious to be the people's champion and knew how to curry favor with Congress.

Jamie Wilkinson rose from behind a single table at the other end of the tavern room and brought me a chair. Before I was quite into it, Gates asked, "Strange, isn't it, that you've inherited General Schuyler's official family?"

I toyed, "Clarkson? Franks?"

"Livingston."

"He has served well in the Northern department. You disapprove?"

"A general is privileged to select his own aides, but I'd say you're a bit overstaffed." Without waiting for my response he continued the offensive. "I understand you submitted a resignation to Congress last month. Just what is your status?"

I answered like a jack-in-the-box, "When General Washington persuaded me to rejoin this army, I requested Congress to suspend action on the resignation. I am determined to ignore the pique that prompted it, the matter of seniority."

"Nevertheless, it is embarrassing to have as my deputy a man outranked by other generals on my staff. I refer to Benjamin Lincoln, who joins us soon." Lincoln was promoted over me from the status of a Massachusetts militiaman.

"I am not to be your deputy?"

"Two continental colonels have asked to serve with you, Morgan and Dearborn. But other veterans of your misbegotten campaign in Canada do not share their enthusiasm." I glared a moment at Wilkinson. "So for the moment, I'm requesting your restraint. You'll receive my order in due course." General Gates rose and moved toward the door.

I was at a loss. He had ambushed me before I could complain as intended. I asked, "And what is your plan, Sir?"

"Plan?"

"I mean of battle!"

"Obviously we must hold Burgoyne, prevent him from joining Clinton, who will be coming up the river valley."

"How would you restrain him?"

"Already done, General. Our defensive positions, staffed with the right officers. We can be supplied. Burgoyne cannot. We win a war of attrition."

I shouted, "Burgoyne should be attacked."

Livingston wrote to Schuyler that a little spirit had broken out between the two generals.

On the 16th of September, Burgoyne was reported two miles off, suffering a severe headache from a boisterous dinner party honoring his mistress, wife of his commissary. Gates was in similar condition without excuse, continuing his masterly inactivity between the Bemis Height and the river. My lads stretched a mile to the west, into the woods. A ravine covered our front; beyond it lay the field called Freeman's Farm. Strong batteries defended our extremities; log breastworks covered the intervals.

Granny awaited Burgoyne with a hot water bottle at his feet and his head wrapped in a vinegar rag. On the 18th, our commander admitted no one; his headache had grown violent. The next morning, Burgoyne was spotted on the move.

I rode out with scouts. It was a crisp, sweet-smelling day, leaves beginning their turn. We heard the roll of drums. Climbing trees, our scouts saw their colors. Polished cannon glared in the autumn sun. They were coming down in three columns, all rigged for a fancy game of war. One column worked through the fallen trees next to the woods, Burgoyne led the center with everything on wheels, and between the road and the river were the Hessians and the Brunswickers.

Rushing back, I thrust myself into the sick man's presence, announced they were marching with a siege train of artillery, and demanded that we surprise them before they could set up.

"Its an open field before our breastworks," Gates answered, "Let them set up. We'll lay them down like wind-rows."

"Burgoyne's no fool. He'll stand off with his heavy guns and demolish our works, while his horse and infantry play around to our left until they can stampede us into the river."

"I suppose you have that direct from Gentleman Johnny?"

"Its what I would do."

"You suggest we charge into them?"

"Before his flanking movement can develop. Burgoyne won't expect a frontal charge. He's too cocky."

"Charge is your strategy?"

"I would send Morgan into the woods and drive them into our frontal attack."

Gates' face tightened. "Our store of powder and ball are near exhausted. We must await new supplies from Albany."

Even Wilkinson knew he lied. "If we wait," the adjutant advised, "they'll bring up cannon for a classic siege. They are expert at that. Our sharpshooters are better in the woods." Jamie had learned something in our Canadian campaign.

Gates dipped his rag into the vinegar bowl, squeezed, and replaced it. At last he said, "Very well. Send out Morgan. Let the game begin."

But I was ordered to remain at his side in the red clapboard tavern. And there would be no frontal attack. He expected Morgan would drive them into the breastworks. We watched the line of riflemen rising and falling like a serpent transversing the gullies. They were slow, seeming to oscillate in place, eerily mute as they trudged. Each bore his load of courage. I knew they were trembling and frightened of the next moment. Tomorrow most of them would be sitting on a moss of rotted logs, odor of powder still in their nostrils, tongues stiff and dry, haunted by memories of their pikes hooked into screaming horses. Or were they just brutes, plough-toughened hands and shoulders yoked in perpetual stupor to their wagons and artillery? The last of the serpent finally disappeared into the woods.

Lobsterbacks floated up from the sea of wheat and moved in wavering lines. The woods came alive with shouts, musket poofs, and the pings of Morgan's rifles. A smell of rotted iron drifted to us. I saw a flurry of red and blue dots clashing helter-skelter and craved to rush forward. With a sweeping gesture I would impose order upon it all. I was their emblem. They would respond to me. And so would Burgoyne, as the Indians did at Stanwix, and St. Leger himself.

Men ran out of the woods into the clearing. Morgan's turkey call sounded and they scuttled back, but I could no longer watch. I stormed out of the little red tavern and called upon Scammel and Cilly to collect their men for an immediate charge. "I want a tight front of 400 yards stuffed with 4000 advancing muskets." As they charged onto the field, I rode back to Gates, almost into his tiny headquarters and yelled for reinforcements, "Now is the moment!"

"No frontal attack."

"We must throw in everything. One strong push at the front will crush them."

"Preposterous." It was Wilkinson's treacherous voice.

"No more troops shall go," Gates called. "We cannot suffer the camp to be exposed. And you, General Arnold, shall return to your tent and stay there."

I obeyed but did not dismount. (My tent was a hut owned by a man named Neilson.) Through my glass, I saw Dearborn's infantry emerge from the wood, responding instinctively to the charge. Morgan's rifles followed. Back and forth they went, the British chasing, then being chased, one dominating the clearance a while, then the other. After each flurry, bodies were thrashing or motionless in the weeds. When I saw Morgan take an unobstructed path to the ravine, I was beside myself to warn him of a trap. A strong force, Fraser's Canadians I think, closed on him. Containing myself no longer, I galloped back to Gates.

He was standing outside his headquarters. "One word, Arnold, and I'll court martial you for flagrant disobedience."

"And what of Morgan's lads?" I shouted.

"The sun is down. Nightfall will end it."

"By God, I'll end it."

Hardly had I remounted when Wilkinson came after with a direct order from General Gates to call our forces off the field.

Tempted to get down and kick him, I realized all would be dark within the hour. I obeyed.

Several times our lads had captured their artillery but were never able to carry it off. Nor could we turn their guns upon them; shrewdly they had removed the linestocks. We lost 300, they perhaps 500. Because they slept that night in the clearing of Freeman's Farm, Burgoyne claimed he beat us. But his army was mauled, except for the Hessians standing on their arms at the river. Another such victory and Burgoyne was done.

In Bemis tavern that night. I urged Gates to continue at sun-up. I fumed and stamped the floor, at last consigning him to hell and storming out.

After burying our dead in the morning fog — throwing officers into separate holes — I read in Gates' general order of the day that I was officially stripped of command. Scammel and Cilly were to report directly to Gates until General Lincoln arrived, Dearborn and Morgan also. His official report of the battle made no reference to a General Arnold. Livingston wrote to Schuyler, "It is evident that our Commander never intended to fight Burgoyne until Arnold urged, begged, and entreated."

When the sentries refused to admit me into headquarters the next evening, I drew my pistol. Gates was dictating to Wilkinson, who looked up and fell backwards over his chair. He was instantly on his feet and drawing away, using his writing board as a shield.

"I want plain answers to plain questions," I demanded.

"You are in the presence of your senior officer."

"Senior be damned." Actually I was not that furious when I started out. "Why did you order me from the field when we were on the point of a rout?"

"You are out of line, General. I've no obligation to explain anything to you. But I will say the battle developed as planned and I would not have a rash subordinate lose the day."

"I'd have won it! And still can, today! They are badly mauled."

"If you do not control yourself, General, I'll be forced to place you under arrest."

"Your official report to Congress did not mention me."

"I report as I see fit."

"What right have you to take Morgan and Dearborn from me?"

"Precisely my right."

"You owe me the courtesy of discussing it."

"I owe you nothing, Arnold. I haven't even the assurance you hold a commission. In fact, I'm informed that Congress has accepted your resignation." He turned to Wilkinson standing at the door. "Colonel, you are witness to this unpleasantness. Mark now, Arnold, I order you to leave my presence at once."

"Immediately! And permanently!"

Gates lips sucked into his mouth; his pinched face was near red against the grey strings of his wig. "I'll prepare a formal pass," he brought out as if all this time we were becalmed at sea, "so that you may leave with impunity ... if you will submit the request in writing."

Retrieving a shred if dignity, I said, "I'll not brook such usage," pushed Wilkinson side, and slammed the door.

"As it is the expressed opinion of the general commanding the army of the North" I wrote, "that I am capable of making no contribution to the victory which our cause demands, I do hereby request formal passes for myself and my aides to return to the headquarters of the main body of the army of the United States."

General Lincoln arrived the next afternoon. He is so fat two men helped him dismount, but like many men of girth, he is congenial. Lincoln regretted my conflict with Gates. My pass also arrived that afternoon, addressed to the president of Congress, John Hancock. It suggested my written request was somewhat insubordinate. I had agreed to a pass to leave my post, not a Congressional inquiry.

Livingston wrote Schuyler, "The reason for the present disagreement is simply this: *Arnold is your friend*. I shall accompany the general. I can no longer submit to the command of a man whom I abhor to my very soul." And Matty wrote, "If Arnold leaves we apprehend a retreat." Indeed so alarmed were the troops and officers at the prospect that they circulated a petition, begging me to stay.

If this were not enough to decide the matter, General Schuyler sent a letter into camp (to Livingston) stating, "Gates will be indebted to Arnold for any glory he may acquire by a victory. But perhaps he is now so very sure of success that he does not wish the other to come in for a share of it." Thus I had no recourse but to announce that no personal consideration would induce me to abandon my lads on the eve of battle. I had pocketed many insults for the sake of my country. I could another.

My decision was applauded through the camp. But no compromise was possible between Gates and me. The rift was too wide. I returned his pass with a word, "Unsuitable." That night Jamie Wilkinson came to me and intimated that if I'd rid myself of the offensive aides or at least Henry Livingston, Gates would change his attitude. "The commander is certain your mind is poisoned by those about you."

It was Jamie's opinion, offered as a gesture of friendship between former comrades, that Gates was on edge about Henry's father, Governor Livingston, and his influence in Congress. If young Livingston were removed, Congress would see that our difficulties resulted from the trouble-making of the governor's spoiled son. I drew myself as straight as possible (Jamie is a touch taller.) "You know me well enough," I told him. "I am hardly the one to sacrifice a friend to that face of clay."

But Livingston, determined to open a way for accommodation, returned to General Schuyler's family in Albany. Daily I awaited the final blow, an order to gather my gear and return to the main army. They were anxious days, pacing before my hut, watching officers galloping up to Gates' little headquarters and rushing off. But Gates was either placated by the sacrifice of my aide or he was intimidated. Though he accused me of murmuring discontent and stuttering sedition through the camp, his order never came.

Let me force the business at hand — Johnny Burgoyne. It is said he rose in the military by marriage with Lady Charlotte

Stanly, daughter of the Earl of Darby, who had considered him with contempt. But he won the old fool's heart for humane treatment of his troops, and for assistance to the King of Portugal against the Spanish Bourbons. A skilled gambler, talented dramatist, and even for a Britisher, uncommonly cocky. He had marched down unopposed and was now setting up on the plains due to Gates' stubborn incompetence.

We watched as Burgoyne extended an entrenchment across Mill Creek (running down the center of Freeman's Farm) all the way to the river. Trusting the water to guard his left, he constructed redoubts on his right. The deserter who gave us this information said many were sick and daily rations were reduced to a loaf of bread and a pound of beef. Poor Englishmen. On the march to Quebec, our lads boiled their wallets.

Burgoyne, however, took courage from my altercation with Gates. And because we lingered in our barracks, he thought us weak. I now wrote Gates, "I am determined to sacrifice my feelings for the public good. It is my duty to inform you that the army clamors for action, and to remind you that militiamen are always threatening to go home. Please do not construe this hint as a wish to command the army and outshine you." Never had I felt so helpless. I watched our brigades march back and forth and practice their fire.

Shortly before noon on October 7, a warm Indian summer day, I was sitting to breakfast in the mess tent where liquor and rations had just been issued, when Wilkinson burst in. "Burgoyne is marching with 1500 men!" He described an advance of Canadians and Brunswickers driven back from a log barn after a hot skirmish. Gates continued eating his ox-heart. The table was silent.

"Shall I go see?" I offered.

After a moment's stare, Gates replied bluntly. "I'm afraid to trust you, Arnold."

"If the lads need no support, I'll not commit."

"You will not commit under any circumstances."

I was allowed to accompany Wilkinson.

Battles of Freeman's Farm 1777

Without exchanging a word, we rode to a hill within 300 yards of them. What seemed Burgoyne's main force had advanced into the wheat field where they were cutting grain for pies. Artillery were moving up behind their right. Other infantry were tiptoeing like thieves through a melon patch. Columns were formed near the height to the west, stretching into the woods beyond the redoubts. We hurried back.

"What is the nature of the ground?" Granny asked his adjutant.

"Their flank rests in the woods."

"What is your opinion?"

"They approach our left wing. Their front is vulnerable."

"And their right?"

Wilkinson shrugged.

"Skirted by a height," I put in.

Gates did not so much as glance at me. To Wilkinson, "You would indulge them?"

"Yes Sir," he snapped.

"Well then," he told his smart adjutant, "order on Morgan."

I paced outside, Davy Franks at my side. We saw Morgan's rifles line up and disappear into the woods. Then Learned's brigade went out — they occupied the breastworks. I thought I saw Scammel and Chilly also go off towards the woods but they were supposed to be with Learned. All were still under my command, officially. I had received no written order.

We heard their cannon, then the single roar of mass fire, our soldiers shouting and returning it. I could see vague undulating lines and imagined each lad, eyes afire in the boiling smoke, gorging himself on it, without water or air ... heedless, sublimely selfless ... animal in a herd without direction. When I saw the first bloodied men carried into the barn, I shouted "Get General Warren." Franks brought up my large brown horse.

Some say I was drunk on air or opium, that I charged out, yelling, "No man will hold me this day." I recall prancing about the camp with great agitation and wrath, turning again and again before headquarters, seeing Gates sitting outside at ease chatting with aides or a messenger reporting from battle, my ear aching to hear them. Silently I begged for an order to join my lads in the clamor. Once Gates glanced up, but didn't see me. I was consumed in anticipation. Some troops were waiting at the ready. I rode up to them as if to bark an order. Regaining my senses, I waved my sword and doubled back. The smell of burned powder filled my nostrils. I dug in my spurs, leaned forward and shouted. But what was I shouting? I cannot say.

By the time Gates sent Major Armstrong after me, it was too late. He never got near enough to speak. That day no order contained me. I charged about as I wished, all commanders yielding to my lead. "It's Arnold," they called as I ran up. I whirled my hat and shouted, "Come on lads, if the day is long enough, they'll be in hell before night." Realizing our enemy was working towards the woods, I galloped back to headquarters. Gates was just emerging, angrily. A bloodied British officer lay on the mattress within. I yelled, "The woods must be defended or the entire camp is lost." He was so mad he didn't hear, fuming to no one, "Never have I met so impudent a son of a bitch." Then he looked up as if surprised. I had no time for challenges. "Morgan can't defend the woods alone."

As one in a daze, "Can't he?"

"You must send relief."

Now Gates came to his senses. "Arnold get off that horse."

(I did not then realize the bloodied soul on the mattress was a prisoner, Sir Francis Clarke. I rode up in the midst of a fiery discussion about the rights of the Colonies to revolt, and Gates had just then stormed outside, angered because Clarke would not concede his argument. His remark, "Never have I met so impudent a son of a bitch," referred not to me but to Sir Francis. It was Gates' frustration with his noble prisoner, who died that night, that allowed the moment's confusion in which I returned to battle.)

I galloped back and ordered a general advance to the enemy right, the woods. That was the move that won the day. Instead of giving battle, they had to take it. Burgoyne drew back.

Had they turned the woods, their artillery would have been near enough to devastate our camp.

They say I criss-crossed lines of fire all afternoon. Dashing about, I spotted General Fraser on a huge grey mount. He had been pushed toward the center where he was reinvigorating his men. When I found Morgan, I asked could he get a sharpshooter in a tree to cut down Fraser. Never before had I issued such an order, but trusted chance of battle. I had uttered a sentence of execution. But wouldn't Fraser do the same if he had the long shooter?

I felt queasy at the sight of Simon Fraser toppling from his high horse in full uniform, medals and sash. Without their leader, the enemy broke and ran to their fortification.

So long as I managed to evade Major Armstrong, I was commander of the field. It was essential to keep moving, flash an appearance, thunder an order, and be gone. I turned to the left again. Morgan was raining steady fire on the Brunswickers defending the redoubts. "Follow me lads."

We concentrated fire on the thin abatis of sharpened logs between the redoubts, then feigned a flanking movement, suddenly shifted direction, and drove through, Learned's brigade following. I directed that he engage the defenders while I led a charge around the redoubt into the sally port. The Brunswickers fled directly into Learned's guns. He merely had to stand and pick them off. Then we had only to turn the captured cannon on the other redoubt and both were ours. But my luck ran out.

I took the wounded soldier in the redoubt for dead, until he rose on his elbow and aimed a musket. I froze. It seemed forever until the burst cut me down. Almost at once Gates' fury rode in. "Do nothing rash," Armstrong commanded. He took the lad's musket and was about to shoot him. "Don't," I called. "He's only doing his duty." Undecided, Armstrong butted him unconscious. I thought to ask for the same, the pain had become so intense.

As they prepared my leg for the litter, followers came into the redoubt. They searched the groaning wounded and dead, stripping the bodies. One suddenly shrieked, "My husband, Lord

Jesus, my poor husband!" Another told her, "Damn your husband. We know you are a whore. You can get another."

Before I blacked out, an emperic appeared and asked my permission to amputate. They had stopped the blood but the leg was useless. If that was all he had to say I'd rather be put on my horse and see the end of the battle.

This hospital in Albany is nothing more than a converted barracks from the border wars. Schuyler tells me Burgoyne surrendered in a field between Stillwater and Saratoga. He chuckled. "Congress is striking a metal for Horatio Gates,"

"They should have cashiered him and struck the metal for Major Armstrong instead. He's responsible for my nimbleness."

"Washington is insisting your seniority be restored."

General Lincoln, shot by a sniper the day after the last battle, is more severely wounded than I, yet he is already walking. "I mend faster," he tells me, "because my mind is calm. Your peevishness would degrade the most capricious of the fair sex." He boasts that he will soon retake the field, then turns and lumbers off as his bulk and wound permit.

I am peevish because week after week, my leg bound to a plank, I anticipate the dispatch that should bring the commission restoring my seniority.

Chapter 10
Observations En Route to New York
1778

Amid clouds of mosquitoes, thousands of Loyalists and cluttering luggage, I find respite in these naked notations.

June 21, 1778.
The peace commissioners who arrived on the 6th found us ready to quit Philadelphia. Sir Henry made no secret of it. Soldiers who married in the town hid in cellars. Desertions are near a thousand.

Wagons of stores and baggage that our transports could not receive extend a line twelve miles long. We are most vulnerable to attack. General Grey is upset that General Clinton did not order the encumbrances destroyed.

At 3 a.m. began the march to New York, the weather warm and calm. A few important Loyalists lingered on to the last. Others came after in a great hurry, encumbered with more baggage.

At 4 o'clock in the morning we marched through Slab Town to the *Black Horse Tavern*, where rebel papers were found warning us to "beware of being Burgoyned." A deserter was executed on the road.

June 26.
Five a.m. General Knyphausen on the march with the entire train of baggage, our refugees not far behind. Sir Henry Clinton confesses the error of dangerously encumbering our operations. But the Americans must traverse bad ground to reach

us, and their ranks would necessarily fall into disorder. Is it the Loyalists or the baggage they want?

July 1.

On the sweltering day of June 28, the rebels attacked our lines near the Monmouth courthouse. We put up a powerful front. Their General Charles Lee quickly fell back and we pursued, until Washington interrupted. He took charge and turned the rebels about. Lee, it is rumored, is suspended from command.

The heat was oppressive. Men on both sides fell dead in the ranks without a wound. The panting Brunswickers swore they would fight no longer in such atmosphere. At 10 p.m. our weary bands joined Knyphausen in the Nut Swamp.

Washington bragged in his general order that he obtained a victory over his Brittanic Majesty's troops. He appointed a party of 200 to bury their slain.

July 11.

Scouts report that Admiral D'Estaing has anchored outside the Hook with twelve ships of the line, six frigates and 4000 French troops. We have six ships of the line, some small craft, and a vast number of merchant transports to receive us. The anger and indignation of our ranks will supply any deficiency in our muster rolls. Mates and masters of the merchant men seek places at the guns among our common sailors. If D'Estaing comes over the bar into the harbor, he will never get out.

Our encampment at Bedford, Long Island seems a village sunk in quicksand, the gable roofs low over our trenches. I am quartered with a Dutchman, Leffert Lefforts, and his silly daughters in a farmhouse that rises by comparison to great heights, a story and a half.

The Lefforts frauleins are in the habit of spoofing British officers to their faces in their native Dutch. But I astounded them, admonishing the young ladies in their own language. Captain Simcoe fancies the plump one.

August 30.
A heavy gale has dispersed D'Estaing's fleet as well as ours. We have intelligence that D'Estaing has notified the rebels he cannot assist in their siege but must proceed forthwith to refit at Martinique. The American generals are seething and the populace are enflamed. Some Frenchmen were severely handled by a Boston mob.

September 1.
General Clinton has revealed to General Grey the plan imposed upon him by the pacification committee. (Officially I am not privy and have sworn my honor to keep the secret.) It is to shift action to the South and to influence the North to a settlement, all grievances met, all rebellious crimes forgiven. He will use the King's purse liberally in this endeavor since the Americans have no reputation for probity. Their shameful thirst for gain, Clinton believes, has relaxed their honesty. "Next to the destruction of Washington's army," he says, "the gaining over of influential officers would be the speediest means of subduing the rebellion. Expenses will be cheerfully remitted." My invitation to advancement.

September 2.
General Grey, eager to provide for me upon his return to England, has pushed me closer to Sir Henry Clinton. We are sailing together on the frigate *Carisfort*. To make the most of this opportunity I have learned what I can of Clinton's history and character. His father, Admiral George Clinton, was royal governor of New York and the builder of Kenilworth. But the peerage is not a house of first magnitude since the Clinton name does not appear among the twenty-five great guardians of Magna Carta. He demonstrated heroism at Bunker Hill, leading reinforcements to bolster the wavering Howe; still he is extremely reserved and unpopular with society.

Shy and morose, no doubt his Excellency is lonely. I am painting his portrait, but am frustrated by hasty observation. I hope to whittle his reserve enough to admit my confidence. Although he holds off, I am sure he is in need of a friend.

September 3.

To General Grey, in my presence, Sir Henry Clinton confided that all means of ending the rebellion were acceptable to the war ministry, including those of terror and destruction as General Grey advocates. But Clinton himself has no taste for it. He suggests that only military installations be destroyed. He set out this evening in the *Galatea* for New York while we stood to the eastward in a fair wind for Buzzard's Bay.

September 7.

The wind does not permit any further movement of the fleet. We took advantage of these circumstances to burn a large privateer on the stocks and to send a small group of boats to burn a vessel upstream. Three or four of the enemy were found bayoneted, one an officer. They had fired at the advance party and were not alert enough to get off.

September 10.

Sailed at 7:00 yesterday morning. The ships could not all get through Quick's Hole before the tide turned, and because of headwinds the fleet did not reach Holmes Hole Harbor in Martha's Vineyard until today. Along the way, the galleys went into Falmouth and cut out two sloops and a schooner.

In the evening a flag of truce with three inhabitants came on board to ask our intentions. They professed peaceful dispositions and readiness to comply with General Grey's orders. He sent them ashore to direct the inhabitants to drive in their sheep and cattle, unless they wished troops to be marched through their island. They were also directed to bring in their arms, or their colonel and captains of militia would be sent as prisoners to New York. General Grey demands 300 oxen, 10,000 sheep and the public money.

September 11.
Twenty vessels arrived from Rhode Island to take in stock. We find it necessary to send small detachments onto the island to accelerate compliance with General Grey's demand.

September 15.
Cattle and sheep have embarked over the last two days while detachments destroyed some salt works and burned vessels found in inlets. A colonel and five captains along with the party of negotiators had to be confined before they fully complied with our demand for arms. The inhabitants are also required to restore two of our men who have deserted, on pain of having a double number of their friends seized.

September 24.
General Clinton requests an accounting of particulars, numbers of vessels and stores of arms and ammunition destroyed or taken, the returns of those killed, wounded or missing. It is apparent he is not interested in military ideals. He wishes, he writes, to settle into New York for a quiescent winter. I must practice more subtlety, a cautious tact.

September 28.
We raided Egg Harbor in New Jersey, destroying several privateers, among them the *Charming Nancy*. Papers show its partly owned by General Benedict Arnold. The hold was empty.

October 13.
We have been two weeks foraging cattle up the North River. On the 29th, a body of rebels appeared beyond Hackensack, lighted fires and threw up entrenchments. At ten that evening, we endeavored to surprise their encampment. Advancing we received intelligence that a whole regiment of their dragoons, commanded by a Colonel Baylor, were asleep at Old Tappan. As at Paoli the year before, General Grey ordered six companies to

remove their flint so that only bayonets and butts would be available to them.

By three in the morning, our light infantry had stolen round the houses and barns where the enemy lay. The whole corps, within six or eight men, were stabbed. Their horses, saddles, accoutrements, etc, fell into our hands. Among the prisoners were a colonel, a captain, and three or four subalterns. The rest died.

November 24.

Major General Grey has departed, recommending me to General Clinton as one possessed of talents in tactful negotiation and intelligence gathering, and as one thoughtful and cordial to all.

November 25.

Unless I can charm his Excellency into an appointment as aide-de-campe, I see my career receding to a minor role of junior captain in the regiment. But General Clinton seems so remote. He does not respect Howe any more than he does Burgoyne. He has most certainly been cold to Howe's former favorites, and perhaps I am considered one of them, having performed several direct assignments for Sir Billy, and lavishly celebrated his departure.

November 27.

I have taken every opportunity to observe his Excellency and have sent my portrait into his office. General Grey found him morose, haughty, churlish even stupid. The portrait shows a prominent nose and tight mouth, determination, deliberate and independent intelligence ... and just a touch of gaiety in the eyes ... one who can be a fellow in liquor and the arms of light women.

November 28.

This evening Lieutenant General Henry Clinton advised me that I am appointed aide-de-campe with the possible provincial rank of major.

Chapter 11

Manuscript Book of Intelligence 1780

I am flattered at being called in the space of three years from a subaltern in the Fusiliers to the favor in which I live with the Commander-in-Chief. Sir Henry has decided I am to be in charge of military intelligence. It is rumored our adjutant may soon return to England, his deputy rise, and that office may be mine, though a mere captain. How can a man of my origin so aspire?

A Philadelphia Marriage

News of a Philadelphia marriage peaks my curiosity. The lady is a Tory, Peggy Shippen, whose father has been judge of the Admiralty as his father before. She is a saucy rogue among the city's belles, pridefully and delightfully spoiled.

But it is the groom who arrests me: Benedict Arnold, at this moment awaiting court martial for a variety of unproven corruptions while military governor of the city. Wherein lies possibility.

All of Europe knows the name, after an inhuman march through the wilderness such as Hannibal would admire, and his conquest of Johnny Burgoyne. And how do these Lilliputians treat such a worthy? They promote others over Arnold, then persecute him with charges as vital as appearing at court with unpowdered hair.

I envision him as a bright barking cocker among American dogs. My pen doodles Arnold without a face, embattled upon a horse, sword flailing, calling, "Follow me." Disabused of one dream — that his fellow Americans are gentlemen — he pursues another, the beautiful Tory belle; the fever of resentment rechanneled into the fervor of courtship. But he has not learned to hide his dreams. So he suffers the contumely of his fellows, chiefly Joseph Reed, president of the Pennsylvania Supreme Council.

Reed has charged Arnold with corruption of his office. According to the *Pennsylvania Packet,* he claims that Arnold permitted *The Charming Nancy* to enter a closed port. I recall the exciting moment a light breeze carried my squadron into Egg Harbor where I boarded the *Charming Nancy* and found its hold barren. Arnold's name was among those on the owners documents.

Other charges are even more minuscule, closing the public shops, sending public wagons to Egg Harbor for transporting cargo from the *Charming Nancy,* and refusing to explain himself. The Council President has publicly pledged the banishing of this despicable Arnold from all positions of honor and trust in the City of Philadelphia.

The Pastor

Entering the pastor's attic room on Wall Street, I was self-conscious of my gleaming red coat and shining black boots. I threw his pay upon a cracked tabletop at the window. He grasped the coins.

"We appreciate the Arnold essay." It extolled the explosive American general now in the fangs of the Supreme Council of Pennsylvania.

"Wine?" responded the reverend Jonathan Odell and was immediately opening a bottle. It was taking bread from the poor. In Philadelphia he wrote essays for Howe in return for a few shillings to support his wife and child in New Jersey. He also received six shillings a day as chaplain to the Pennsylvania Loyalists. In New York, Odell continues as occasional hack and pastor. His mouth folds as if his teeth are gone, the eyes droop at the edges. Yet his countenance is uncannily happy, not like a fool's but seasoned beyond sadness and remarkably alert for one so frequently imbibing.

The attic was not particularly hot but the wine, a touch bitter, brought out a sweat. My neck was damp.

"Remember our slender friend, Stansbury?" the parson asked.

"The crockery dealer. A worse poet never existed."

A ditty immediately followed about a drunken wastrel. "The Americans arrested him for it."

"No, Parson, the Americans arrested him for singing "God Save the King. At a party in '76 in his china shop on Front Street."

I lifted my glass and we drank to Joseph Stansbury.

"Stalwart of the Church and King Club," said the pastor.

"Could hardly keep a straight face." Stansbury seldom spoke without a giggle, and took to calling General Howe 'the carpet knight.' "Didn't he sign their oath of allegiance?"

"Duress."

"He is familiar with General Arnold's case?"

"Most sympathetic. Even considers him movable."

"Indeed?"

Anonymous

My first effort was to the crockery dealer, invoking Odell's name. On the paper my words were awkward, almost incoherent. Then I decided to enclose a letter for Peggy, but why not Arnold himself? I would stir the humanity most certainly concealed in the general's tough and dash. The object was to inspire means for achieving a just peace. Yet the letter must hit upon Arnold's practical instincts as a man of trade. My concentration was encumbered by irony; such a momentous act inspired by two buffoons, the pastor and his slender friend, and unfolding without an ounce of forethought or permission. The lamps were lit before I copied out a satisfactory draft:

"Shall your provinces flourish, as in former days, under the protection of the most puissant nation on earth? Or will you pursue that shadow of liberty that escapes your hand even in the act of grasping it! And if ever obtained, how soon could that liberty turn into licentiousness?

"Our peace commissioners have offered Americans their own Parliament. All their laws shall be the production of this assembly. Commerce in every part of the globe shall be as free to the people of the thirteen colonies as to the English of Europe. Everything urges us to put a conclusion to dissent, not less detrimental to the victors than to the vanquished.

"Render then, brave General, an important service to your country. Your troops are perishing in misery. They are badly armed, half naked, and crying for bread. Your fields are untilled, trade languishes, learning dies. The neglected education of a whole generation is an irreparable loss. Your youth, such as survive, have lost the vigor of their prime or are maimed in battle; the greater part bring back to their families the idleness and corrupt manners of the camp.

"Let us put an end to so many calamities. You and ourselves have the same origin, the same language, the same laws. We are inaccessible on our island; and you, the masters of a vast and fertile territory. The ocean is our home. We pass across it as a monarch traversing his dominions, each bearing the stamp of liberty.

"How destructive, then, to break forever the links and ties of a friendship a hundred and fifty years old. I appeal to you, illustrious Arnold, reunite us in equality so together we may bind the universe, not by arms and violence, but ties of commerce, the lightest and most gentle bonds that human kind can wear."

After the letter was given into Odell's hand, I realized it was not signed. For two guineas he guarantees the crockery man will carry it to the general.

The Crockery Man

Portraits of George and Charlotte, put up on his Majesty's birthday, still decorate King's Head Tavern. On the opposite wall, the devil hovers over the President of Congress, whose face is a blur — the Presidents change so often. Also hanging there is a print of a British tar trampling the thirteen stripes, and beside it an article from Rivington's *Gazette* with the heading, CON-

GRESS ARE THE PEOPLE'S PIMP. I read, "In America scum rises to the top. Is it wiser to spend your precious time scouring? Or tending your own garden?"

I slipped past loud singers at the pianoforte and approached Odell at a corner table. The singers were shouting, "So while we can stand, the flagon command ..." when a tall one in greatcoat and brimmed hat, unseasonable for the warm May morning, turned away and followed me. I was no sooner seated than he was standing before us, body unbent to its considerable height. I recognized the puckered face. It was the poetic crockery dealer of Philadelphia. "Stansbury!"

"Stevens," he corrected me, then with furtive glances he unbuttoned his coat, exposing a white shirt with wilted ruffles, and sat. "I am Jonathan Stevens, merchant."

Odell said, "Mr. Sevens has had an arduous trip." He asked Stansbury, "You remember John Anderson?"

"Indeed, although we had little opportunity for trade in Philadelphia."

Confounded, I turned to the parson, "Odell —"

"Osborne, if you please. John Osborne, merchant. We are all merchants here."

Stansbury giggled.

Odell had asked me to the tavern, promising a surprise. Finally perceiving the game, I said, "I must insist on my own name," and one from a popular fiction popped to mind, "I am Joseph Andrews."

Stansbury was nervous. "Is there a less conspicuous place? New York crawls with Washington's agents."

"You have taken the oath," the pastor reminded him.

"That does not impress Joseph Reed." Stansbury's sonorous voice was reduced to a whisper, "I am already suspected and if my shop remains closed too many days —"

"Then let us be brief," I cut in.

"Briefly," Stansbury sighed as a man gathering breath for a speech. "General Monk sent for me —"

"Monk?" I knew of no American general with that auspicious name.

Stansbury giggled and continued, "Actually, it was his exquisite wife who came to me, pretending interest in my china. She is impressed with the idea of returning to loyalty. The Supreme Executives of Pennsylvania are to her husband as the French clergy to Quebec, 'Machines,' she calls them, 'by which the common people are governed.'" Stansbury glanced about.

I could hear only some of his sibilant words. "Speak up."

Again Stansbury cast about and then with a trifle more force, whispered, "General Monk, of course, has concerns. His property. Losses to be incurred. Madam conjectures they can live on the gratitude of the English, if necessary in Britain. He insists on indemnification of all that is risked."

"Insists?" It was much too loud. With some modulation I continued, "Stansbury, am I to understand you have begun negotiation without so much as hello to General Clinton?"

"General Monk is an impetuous man. And it was Sir Henry Clinton who began the negotiation. An anonymous letter was received. No signature was needed, of course. But it was an alarmingly open message."

"General Arn... — General Monk was not appreciative?"

"Apprehensive. Not so his lady. She admires the writer's style and inspires her husband. It is her opinion that our General Monk must envision things heroically before he can act upon them."

"Much like his original." My excitement was enhanced by an image of the maligned American hero as General Monk, Oliver Cromwell's righteous lieutenant who returned to loyalty upon the dictator's death and led the zealots back to King Charles. They made him Duke of Albemarle. Were Peggy's hopes similar? Lord and Lady Arnold? "You claim he is apprehensive, but a moment ago you said he was impetuous?"

"Apprehensive that the British will falter. He wants assurance you will persist until you win. If that can be given, he is most impetuous, eager to restore a responsible government, destroy the usurped authority of Congress, and, as he says, 'stop this insane bloodshed of brothers.'"

"Specifics?" I blurted. "Conditions?"

Now Stansbury lost his control. He was no longer able to modulate his voice into the rhythms of polite conversation, though he still whispered. "The primary condition is to be assured of your sincerity, that no thought is entertained in New York or London of abandoning your objective in America. In no circumstances will you concede independence."

"On the contrary, we are adamant. The most powerful means are anticipated for this end."

Stansbury began to list Arnold's terms and requirements for compensation, but a disheveled grey-beard brushed by and he abruptly stopped, "This place will not do."

"Shall we continue at my place?" Odell offered. The crockery dealer approved. Outside I said I'd meet them at the attic and ran off to headquarters.

His Excellency had retired with Miss Blundel and was not to be disturbed. Perhaps the moment was premature. After all, I had come away from Stansbury with little information, not nearly enough to justify unsettling Sir Henry. The proposal was so sudden it confused me. I was rushing into determination before I had time for deliberation.

Back at Odell's, Stansbury had grown more jittery; his shirt ruffles seemed to shake. He refused Odell's wine. Pretending a tranquil air, I said, "Whatever General Monk may require, our liberality will be evinced the moment we receive his good offices. Of course, General Clinton will have to be consulted."

"May I ask what service General Monk is to render?"

I was unprepared. "Whatever he chances upon."

"Nothing in particular?"

I felt the perspiration at my temples and neck. Suspiciously, I looked at Odell, who turned away. Stansbury noticed the exchange. "General Monk has not sent me here seeking intelligence," he said quickly, "but offering it."

I returned to the tack of compensation, "If any important blow should be struck upon the strength of your general's cooperation, his reward will equal the value of his service." I knew I had said little and silently continued to search for substance.

"And in case of exposure," the crockery man wished to know, "what indemnity?"

"If his efforts are foiled and flight necessary?"

Stansbury nodded.

"Then the cause in which he suffers binds itself to indemnify his losses." The flourish of my language impelled me onward, beyond my authority. But surely Sir Henry would offer as much, even more. I added, "And we shall receive him with the honors his conduct deserves."

Stansbury inquired further of the services desired. Finally, he asked directly, "Shall General Monk join the British army or remain an American general?"

A General Monk would lead his forces back to loyalty, an act desired above all. But Arnold had no forces, and his welcome in the British army was a decision even beyond Sir Henry's powers. "For the moment he can be of great assistance by providing us the contents of dispatches, the channels through which they pass, the discussions of Congress, plans of foreign abettors, military organizations and the like. He might seize papers and send them. Especially valuable are numbers and positions of troops, commands in different quarters, points where magazines may be accumulating."

A churning started in my stomach, but it dissipated in renewed excitement when Stansbury asked, "How shall we communicate?"

Codes, of course! I love the intricacy of puzzles and mysterious arrangement. Among Odell's books piled along the walls, I spotted Blackstone's *Commentaries*. "Ah, the long book." I brought it over to Odell's cracked table and asked for pen and paper.

Stansbury sat silently, his face consumed in curiosity, while Odell drank and I worked. In a few minutes I produced a set of instructions for the general in Philadelphia. I read aloud: "Procure a copy of *Blackstone's*. Three numbers shall make a word. The first is the page in the book, the second is the line, and the third is the word."

"But how shall we compose words not in the book?"

I thought a moment. "Ah, by using the first letter of each line. And the sign for that reading —" confusion had spread over Stansbury's features. "— Nevermind. We'll just make the words invisible, the ink to be discovered by a process. F for fire, A for acid. The code letter placed in a corner. Must I write that also?"

"I can remember."

"Good." I held the sheet of instructions to the candle.

Sir Henry Clinton

His Excellency was vexed. "And what troops does Madam Monk command?" He went to his chest of spirits and poured from a crystal flask into squat glasses. "London weather has changed again."

I sipped. "Are we no longer to persuade their generals?"

Sir Henry sank back into his chair and nodded sententiously. "Treason doth never prosper, know the reason?"

A familiar ditty, "'If it prosper, none dare call it treason.' Sir John Harrington. But his wisdom was limited."

"Oh?"

"Elizabeth permitted him to construct and install a privy with running water in her chamber."

"The Ajax."

"Then you know the story?"

"Upon the pull of a chain, the noisy water frightened the Queen's innards. 'Take a patent and sell it to the Irish,' she told Sir John, 'Your jest will be the ruin of my bowels.'" Sir Henry bellowed. "You are the man for me, Andre. Let's another." I poured and abruptly his mood changed. "Lord North wants a quick end. One massive blow. So what shall we do? A blow requires a target. Washington's evasions provide none. I suppose we must go south. Cornwallis reports the Southern rebels less enthusiastic." His head sank.

Sir Henry is the subject of mounting criticism in the ministry. Rumors place Cornwallis as more representative of military tradition. A remark in Congress has reached London ears, "As fertile as England is in the production of blockheads, they cannot easily send us a greater blunderbuss." His Excellency poured one for himself.

"And what of Arnold?" I blurted.

"Arnold?" He mulled the name. "If not for that dumbbrave apothecary, we'd have broken them. No need to go south."

"I mean, Sir, his overture."

Clinton shifted restlessly in his chair as if I were an annoyance. "We always value intelligence, if we can trust it. But as a General Monk leading the wayward home? He is in disgrace and not likely to be further employed. Without a command, Arnold is a poor investment."

Packet From the Parson

Today, I left Sir Henry on the tip of Long Island and returned to headquarters. Ostensibly Sir Henry is conferring with the fleet. At Colonel Abraham Gardiner's mansion, we played quoits and drank sanguiri.

The sun still bakes New York's streets; the stench from Canvas Town and the prisons is keen. Officers escort their ladies up the East River or take the Brooklyn ferry to the Hempstead track. Captain Beckwith, who assumed my duties, brought in a packet delivered by two young men who were returning a favor for the reverend Jonathan Odell. They told Beckwith the packet was received from Odell's "slender friend." Bound in oily black paper, it glows on my desk. It is sealed and tied with hemp, clumps of dried earth between the hemp and the paper. No words anywhere. I shift it, hand to hand, prolonging the excitement.

Three sheets are folded on within the other. The outermost is Odell's: "I am mortified to death, having just received a letter from Stevens. Perceiving it contained an invisible page for you, I assayed it by the fire. To my inexpressible vexation, the paper had got damp on the way. The solution spread to make the writing an indistinguishable blot, except for the date. It was the 21st, which I deem is before he received mine, so all is not lost. I hourly await his reply.

"I should not have taken the liberty, but my joy was such that I flew to the fire. Since toasted paper becomes to brittle to bear folding, I shall make it a rule to carefully transcribe all future messages before sending them on. Permit the *parson* to conclude with his earnest prayers for your health and glory."

The second sheet is apparently the expected reply from Stansbury, but in Odell's hand, "The confusion of a town meeting has banished me to Morrestown for preservation." Had we detained him too long? Reading on, I discovered the crockery dealer had over-reacted to a noisy parade of militia and townsmen, "disgruntled by the high price of flour and depreciating money. You know the apathy I have for thunder. So I have sought temporary shelter here in New Jersey. The tall trees and high buildings which make my dwelling in Philadelphia dangerous in stormy weather are not to be met here."

Stansbury also informed Odell that "however impatient your Lothario, Monk is at the present unavailable. Convince him of your sincerity and you may rely upon it, our most sanguine hopes will be surpassed. Otherwise both your credit and mine will suffer greatly."

Why would Odell copy out the last two lines? Why would he want me aware of their conniving? To strengthen my commitment? Or is the parson just empty-headed? It matters little. The letter is signed "Yorick." And I am Lothario. Such is Stansbury's humor. But impatience? If so, its nothing to match that of my plotting agents. I envision frenzied correspondence, their messengers rowing back and forth between South Amboy and Prince's Bay like furies in the black of night.

Arnold's letter is dated May 23 and signed M_G_A_. Has he forsaken General Monk, or is he just careless? "Our friend Stevens acquaints me that my proposals are agreeable to S_H_C_." Examples of intelligence follow, in the same order as I requested: "Gen W. and the army move to the North river as soon as forage can be assured; Congress will give up Charleston if attempted —" But how can Arnold be aware of our intentions in the South? Odell is a leaky vessel to be sure. "They want arms, ammunition, and men to defend Charleston. Three or four thousand militia are the most that can be mustered to fight in any emergency." Perhaps Arnold is not the author. If Stansbury, these details could be invented. Even if Arnold, they could be feigned.

The rest was preoccupied with security and reward. "I will cooperate when an opportunity offers, and as life and everything are at stake I will expect some certainty, my property here secure and revenue equivalent to the risk and service done. I cannot promise success; I will deserve it." Is the principal talking or the agent? The final statement induced another doubt. "Could I know S_H_C_'s intention, he should never be at a loss for intelligence." All a scheme to learn our campaign plans? I know about Arnold's deception of St. Leger at Fort Stanwix. Even his postscript could be a clever stratagem: "Madame A. presents you her particular compliments."

"Sir: The most essential service for wresting this country from ruin would be to reveal the counsels of its rulers. Or could you obtain a command? The rest you must understand. As to a general project against the whole army, could anything take place on the west side of the North River? We would be glad to have your sentiments on this head."

Foolhardy indeed to send such questions. Clinton has not authorized opinion, nothing more than intelligence. Still, why not express the notions flowing in my head? For Sir Henry's appraisal. Questions to be asked of Arnold, but really suggestions for my commander.

"If a considerable corps marches into New England, Washington will cross the North River and hasten to attack. Could you command Washington's troops? A chain of connivance could be artfully laid to multiply difficulties and baffle resources. At such an hour, with the rebel army most boisterous and everyone intent on its fate, the seizing of Congress could decide the business. A few ships might assist in bringing off the Congress or increasing the general confusion on the coast. If added to this, an expedition from Canada destroyed Fort Pitt, and 6000 militia joined in a project to defeat Detroit? Could General Schuyler be encouraged to lead an uprising near Albany (already impatient with their present rulers)? And perhaps hand over the forts at West Point? What resources would remain?

I envisioned Arnold secretly directing the host of rebel leaders in a concerted movement against the rebellion everywhere at once, and finished with a direct recommendation to Sir Henry: "May Arnold be promised provisional major general? He deserves his own rank in the British army."

When General Clinton returned, I was pleased that his pinched face was somewhat relaxed. But it came together again as he studied my propositions and speculations.

"Of course," he said. "If Arnold gained a command and turned it over with thousands of troops. And there was no trap."

"Then I may send a more cogent copy of this letter?"

"Permit me," Sir Henry said.

The approved letter bears Sir Henry's dictates with little correction. Bluntly, it tells Arnold that his Excellency cannot reveal his intentions but that he should not infer thereby any lack of confidence. Further, "General Clinton begs you to observe that *you proposed* the delivery of your country. A conspicuous command in your hands would enable us in one shining stroke to accelerate the ruin to which the usurped authority is verging. Both riches and *honors* would be derived from such service."

Before giving the letter to Odell, I added my own instruction: "Join the army, accept a command, be surprised, be cut off — in the course of maneuver for instance. A complete service of this nature, involving a corps of five or six thousand men, would be rewarded with twice as many thousand guineas."

Moore or Gustavus?

Gazettes note the further postponement of General Arnold's court martial, along with his response to Washington: "If your Excellency thinks me criminal, for heaven's sake let me immediately be tried and, if found guilty, executed ... delay in the present case is worse than death."

Does Arnold refer to his possible return to loyalty? The last correspondence is not encouraging. Stansbury writes:

"I delivered Gustavus your letter. It is not equal to his expectations. He expects to have your promise that he shall be indemnified for loss in case of detection, specifically, ten thousand pounds."

Sir Henry is evasive. Odell, of course, urges me to pursue. "The court postponed a second time, Mr. Moore should be eager to bursting."

Irritated, I ask, "Is it Moore or Gustavus?"

"As long as Stansbury stays in Moorestown it's Moore."

"Are you sure we're corresponding with Arnold?"

Odell nodded, "Or Madam."

"Perhaps too many parties are involved."

"Only Stansbury and myself, in addition to Mrs. Moore."

"Moore to you and Gustavus to me ... well ... do you have any idea why they've grown indifferent?"

"According to Stansbury, Mrs. Moore finds our style laconic, the general finds no attention paid to his request."

"Perhaps they await the outcome of his court martial? And keep us on a string which they'll pull if it is negative? Worse than death?"

"But Mrs. Moore retains a vivid interest. She's sent a list of articles, and will pay for the whole with gratitude."

The list was addressed to a Major Giles at Flatbush:

18 yards wide or 22 yards narrow pale pink pantua
 1 piece broad pale pink ribbon
 6 yards fine black sattinet for shoes
 1 piece diaper for napkins
 1 pair neat spurs
 1 piece clouting diaper

The script was in her hand. I studied the items for clues. Ribbons are ties. And shoes and spurs, fine and neat? The diapers surely mean a beginning. I said, "Our offer is too fanciful and not direct, not neat. They seek better ties, but are not discouraged. We are only at the beginning."

"The diapers are what they appear," Odell answered. "For Madonna and babe."

"With child? Peggy?"

"According to Stansbury."

I took a moment. "And who is Major Giles?"

"Aquila Giles, captured at Brandywine, paroled and now married to a Loyalist on Long Island. He shops through the lines. If I may say, the message is that she wishes and therefore Mr. Moore wishes the correspondence to continue. He is playing the role of offended one, she the mediator. And they want a reply. The messenger is waiting." The parson laughed. "He was detained by some embarrassments along the way and is most nervous."

I glanced again at the list. "This is really intended for the person addressed?" Odell nodded and I tossed the list into a drawer. "You may tell the messenger I'll answer in my own time."

Arnold Names His Price

Sir Henry speculated. "Perhaps Arnold's horse gallops in both directions at once. How do you think?"

"So long as the charges remain, they poison what he holds most dear. Suspended honor is lost honor, worse than death."

The commander grunted. "Hardly a British concern. Can he deliver troops?"

"Then I am to press further?"

"If you are sure it is Arnold, and that he is sanguine. Not a deception plotted by Washington. What is his price?"

"He asks twenty thousand pounds, half that as indemnity."

"Tell him appropriate sums will be forthcoming, but they must be accounted for. Real advantage must appear to justify the expenditure. We'd pay highly for West Point."

I encoded a message that assured Arnold no hesitation remains on our part, but money cannot be offered without accounting, and therefore, "Permit me to prescribe a little exertion. Procure an accurate plan of West Point, with the new roads, etc, an account of what vessels, gunboats or galleys are in the North River, the weight of metal they carry, the army as brigaded with the commands, and so on, where stores and shipping might be destroyed." All of which was beyond prudence, if he were in fact undecided or acting double.

I went on, "The only method of complete conviction on both sides and of arranging important operations is a meeting. Would you assume a command and enable me to see you? I am convinced a conversation of a few minutes would satisfy you entirely and give us equal cause to be pleased. Above all, Sir, let us not lose time or contract our views which, on our part, have become sanguine."

Stansbury responded, "I have had an interview with Mr. Moore. He remarked that your letter contained no reply to his terms. However sincerely he wishes to serve his country in settling this unhappy contest, it would be unjust to his family to hazard his all and part with a certainty for an uncertainty."

Imagine a soldier like Arnold bound in domesticities. I envisioned Peggy, her thin waist swollen, and the lame hero gimping about to serve each piquant desire. Continuing Stansbury's note, however, I realized all was not lost. "He hopes to rejoin the army in about three weeks, and will if possible contrive an interview. I wished him to put pen to paper, but he said, 'you have my sentiments...'"

I took her shopping list from the drawer and sent for Major Aquila Giles, then wrote:

"Madame, Major Giles is so good as to take charge of this letter, which is meant to solicit your remembrance, and to assure you that my respect remains unimpaired by distance or political broils. It would make me happy to become useful to you here.

"You know the Mischianza made me a complete milliner. Should you not have received supplies for that department, I shall be glad to enter into the whole detail of capwire, needles, gauze, etc, and to the best of my abilities, render services from which I hope you infer a zeal to be further employed. Your humble servant, John Andre."

Acting Adjutant General

Sir Henry himself brought the news. I read in Lord Rawdon's delicate hand: "Having no longer the honor of sharing confidence with your Excellency, I request permission to resign this post effective this day. With your permission I shall rejoin my Irish Volunteers who are now in convoy to North Carolina."

Amazing! Advancement not to deputy but to adjutant general itself. At Sir Henry's suggestion, Lt. Colonel Stephen Kemble, current deputy, proposed to rejoin his Sixteenth Regiment somewhere in the West Indies, provided that I pay him three hundred pounds annually. I can hardly look back upon my steep rise without feeling giddy.

Peggy Shippen's letter also arrived today. "Mrs. Arnold presents her best respects to Captain Andre, much obliged to him for his very polite and friendly offer of being serviceable. Major Giles is so obliging as to promise to procure what trifles Mrs. Arnold wants in the millinery way. She begs leave to assure Captain Andre that her friendship and esteem for him is not impaired by time or accident. Mrs. Arnold."

I crumpled her letter and threw it into the fire. The paper fell just short of the flame. Retrieving it, I smoothed the wrinkles and read the letter again. Were they not dismissing me? And the entire enterprise? What made them shift? And oh Lord, what face can I show Sir Henry?

At the evening's celebration for me, I turned from the toasting to inform the pastor, "Our business with Mr. Moore is concluded."

Notices and Transactions

From the *North Carolina Observer,* December 28, 1779;

ARNOLD: ACQUITTAL and REPRIMAND

...on the unauthorized use of military wagons, the court found Arnold's intentions honorable; he had no design of defrauding, injuring, or impeding the public service, but considering the delicacy attending his high station, they are of the opinion that his action was imprudent and improper. The judgment is of venial error only, but the sentence is nevertheless, a reprimand to be delivered publicly by General George Washington.

To Mr. Moore, May 26, 1780   F

Dear Sir — Stevens is taken aback, having arrived in this city and discovering no one in charge. S_H_C_, and his adjutant have yet to return from Carolina. Nor was General Knyphausen in attendance at headquarters. Hearing the continentals are without horse to draw artillery, the Brunswicker chased after them. In the march of a day, he's cost Britain more men than the entire Carolina campaign. He flounders still in New Jersey.

Captain Beckwith received Mr. Stevens' communication and finally procured a response, to wit: General Knyphausen will take the first opportunity of informing S_H_C_, and in the meantime feels happy cultivating the connection. Two rings have been procured, exactly alike, one of them sent to Mr. Moore by Mr. Stevens.

Your most obedient servant,
James Osborne

...

Major General Arnold, June 4, 1780

Dear Sir — The enclosed is a draft of a proclamation addressed to the inhabitants of Canada. You will be pleased to put this into the hands of a printer whose secrecy may be trusted. Have him strike off a proof sheet with the utmost dispatch, which you will send me for correction. We shall want at least 500 copies. The printer is not on any account to reserve a copy himself or to suffer one to get abroad.

I am your most obedient servant,
George Washington

...

G. Beckwith Ring, June 7, 1780   A
Executor to the late John Anderson, Esq.
(in the care of John Osborne, to be left at the Rev. Odell's)

Sir — Forgive my impatience with this cipher, and its corruption. I write in haste. The Commander-in-Chief has sent

me a proclamation in order to have a number of copies printed and sent to Canada. Its purpose will be transmitted to you by Mr. Stevens to whom I have communicated it.
Tomorrow I go to camp. Will be in Morristown the 12th. King's Ferry the 16th. If I meet a person in my mensuration who has the token (ring) agreed upon, you may expect every intelligence in my power. When fully authorized to treat, I wish to have a conference with an officer in whom we can place a mutual confidence.
       Moore

...

To James Osborne, June 16, 1780 F
Sir — Mr. Moore thinks it strange no steps are taken on your part to come to a settlement. He has been waiting for a very explicit answer to his of June 7, and hopes to arrange an interview with some proper businessman as nothing can be done without it.
We have confided certain observations to G.B. Ring, i.e. that six thousand French troops and three or four thousand rebels are being committed to Canada, but we suffer qualms about this information. Would Washington take so little notice of previous experience as to waste such a force against Canada? Mr. Moore suspects Washington is feigning. But if he does not intend to again invade Canada, why has he ordered a Philadelphia printer to make up 500 copies of a proclamation for distribution among the *habitants*? Is there no reliable printer in all of Jersey? Mr. Moore is suspicious. Perhaps Washington counts on Moore to spread the word and witlessly further his true intention, which, in the absence of S_H_C_, he believes is an attack on New York.
     Your most humble servant,
      Jonathan Stevens

...

The Arnold/Andre Transcripts

Continental Army General Order of the Day, August 3rd, 1780
    Major General Benedict Arnold will proceed to West Point and take command of that post, its garrison and all its dependencies from Fishkill to King's Ferry.
    General George Washington

...

To Jonathan Stevens, June 24, 1780   F
(to be left at the Crockery Shop)
    We are upset with your blatant and dangerous disregard of proper business form. I have passed on your perception that New York is a more likely place of business nowadays than Canada. We are pleased that Mr. Moore will soon be in a position to take advantage. Do not be concerned that Mr. Anderson pays you no mind. He does, though Moore is unaware. Advise patience. Now back from their business venture, they are busy extracting their kraut from his expensive folly.
    Your most obedient servant,
    James Osborne

...

To Mr. Moore, Philadelphia, July 24, 1780   A
    Your offer is agreeable, provided the quantity of goods and stores you mentioned are delivered. You must not suppose in case of failure, we would leave you a victim, though indemnity is impossible. Cash is paid for goods received. But in every possible event you will have no cause for complaint. Essential services shall be rewarded profusely, far beyond the stipulated indemnification. Everything may be settled to mutual satisfaction when the projected interview takes place. Mr. Anderson is willing himself to effect the meeting in whatever manner may at the time appear eligible.
    Your humble servant,
    John Anderson, merchant

...

Mr. John Anderson, Merchant, July 28, 1780   A
To the care of James Osborne (to be left at the Rev. Odell's)
    Sir — I hope to procure for you an interview in a few days with Mr. Moore when you will be able to settle your commercial plan agreeable with all parties. Mr. Moore retains the opinion that his first proposal is by no means unreasonable. He expects when you meet you will be fully authorized from your house to close with it and that the risks and profits of the co-partnership may be understood.

    A speculation at this time might be easily made to some advantage with ready money, but there is not the quantity of goods at market which your partner seems to suppose, and the number of speculators below, I think, will be against your making an immediate purchase. I apprehend goods will be in greater plenty and much cheaper in the course of the season. Both dry and wet are much wanted and in demand at this juncture. Some quantities are expected in this part of the country very soon.

    Mr. Moore flatters himself that in the course of ten days he will have the pleasure of seeing you. He requests me to advise you that he has ordered a draft on you in favor of our mutual friend Stevens for 300 pounds — which you will charge on account of tobacco. I am on behalf of Mr. Moore and Co.
               Your most obedient servant,
                       Gustavus

...

John Anderson, Trader. July 30, 1780   A
(to be delivered directly by messenger)
    Sir — Impatient of your reply, and suspecting the persons we employ deceive us, I hasten this further message to you. Your indifference to my valuable offer suggests it has not been properly received. Perhaps the messenger considers editing his duty. Another mercury carries this, a Mary McCarthy on her way to the British lines with her two children. She understands you are an American secret agent acting as trader with the British.

I am sending the following letter to Colonel Elisha Sheldon, in charge of the outpost at North Castle:

"We are trying to establish a line of intelligence of enemy movements. In this regard, expect a stranger, a Mr. John Anderson, a surreptitious trader who is a secret agent in the American service. He will come seeking a Mr. G. Notify me as soon as he or his letter arrives."

If a mutual confidence between us is wanting, our correspondence ought to end. If not, I await your assurance.

                Gustavus

...

To Major John Andre, August 3, 1780

To be frank I am apprehensive about entrusting the proposed mission to my best advisor, friend, and bosom confidant. Though success in this dangerous undertaking might provide the personal triumph that would impress the ministry in London and result in your permanent appointment to the rank of major and the high office you now hold, I forbear.

Colonel Robinson, whose confiscated house is now headquarters for General Arnold, is the most obvious choice as agent. He will probably go with the flag himself. If you must go, it should only be as an inconspicuous member of the party.

        Lt. General Henry Clinton

...

Colonel Elisha Sheldon, North Castle, August 5, 1780

I am told my name is made known to you and that I may hope for your indulgence in permitting me to meet a friend near your outpost. I will endeavor to go with a flag, which will be sent to Dobb's Ferry on Monday next, the 11th at twelve o'clock, when I shall be happy to meet Mr. G.

Should I not be allowed to go, an officer who is to command my escort can speak on the affair. No distinction need

be made between us. I should rather my friend undertake the innocent affair in question than neglect it.
John Anderson, Merchant

...

To Colonel Sheldon, North Castle, August 10, 1780
I am mystified by Mr. Anderson's statement, as you must be, that an officer might represent him. I suspect my actual letter to him has been intercepted and the reply you received, coming as Mr. Anderson's, is counterfeit. Nevertheless I intend to be at Dobb's Ferry on Monday and meet the flag, whoever comes with it. I have promised Mr. Anderson your protection, and that he shall return in safety.   Mr. G.

...

For the Commander, August 12, 1780
We proceeded along the eastern shore through the bleak neutral ground. Approaching Dobb's Ferry, our party halted a little inland so we might be hidden from the river. We observed the *Vulture* at anchor and a gunboat prowling back and forth like a fenced dog.
We waited hour after hour astride our mounts, but Arnold did not show. Perhaps our fierce prowlers kept him at bay. When darkness fell, we returned to our lines.
Acting Adjutant General,
Major John Andre

...

To John Anderson, August 15, 1780
(to be left at the Rev. Odell's)
My partner and I have 1000 on hand for speculation and can raise 1500 more in a few days. Add to this, I have some credit. Our boss will be at King's Ferry Sunday evening next on his way

to Hartford. He will lodge at Peekskill. You can judge of the purchase to be made.
Gustavus

...

Aboard the *Vulture*, August 17, 1780
To Major General Arnold
Dear General: I am persuaded from the humane and generous character you bear that could I be granted a meeting you would readily accede to my request, pertaining to the residence you occupy. But for prudential reasons I dare not explain the matter further.
Most humbly,
Colonel Beverly Robinson

...

To Colonel Beverly Robinson, August 19, 1780
Dear Colonel — I am informed that any application respecting private affairs is made to the civil authority of the state. If you have proposals of a public nature of which I can officially take notice, you may depend on it that the greatest secrecy shall be observed.
His Excellency General Washington will lodge here on Saturday night next, and I will lay before him any matter his old friend may wish to communicate.
B. Arnold, Major General

...

Aboard the *Vulture*, August 19, 1780
To Major General Arnold,
Sir — I have not the least reason to expect any favor from the civil authority after seeing the laws they have passed respecting me and my family. Had I known General Washington was nearby I should certainly have made application to him, as I flatter myself I should be allowed very reasonable indulgence. I beg my

best respects may be presented to him, and I return many thanks for your polite letter and civil expression to me.
>Your most humble servant,
>Beverly Robinson

P.S. I'll wait here till tomorrow night if upon reconsideration, I may be permitted to see you, at any place you please.

...

Colonel Robinson, August 20, 1780
This will be delivered by Mr. Joshua Smith who will conduct you or your adjunct to a place of safety. Neither Mr. Smith nor any other person shall be made acquainted with your proposals. I take it for granted Colonel Robinson will not propose anything that is not for the interest of the United States as well as himself.
>I am, Sir, etc.
>B. Arnold

Enclosed on a paper scrap: "Gustavus to Anderson."

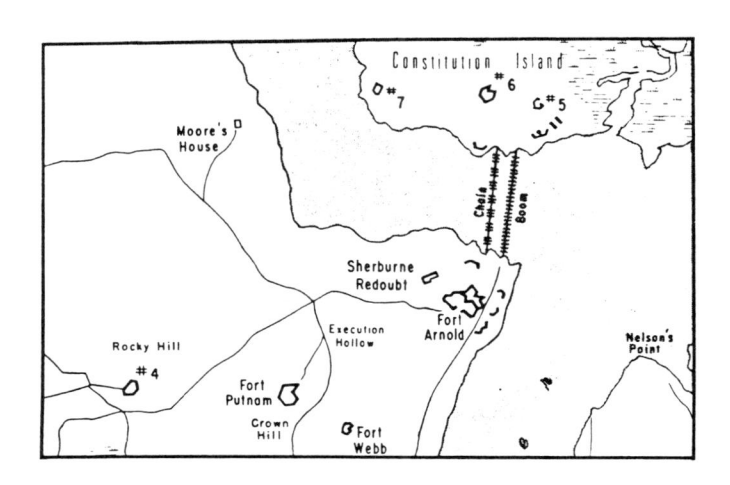

West Point Defenses 1780

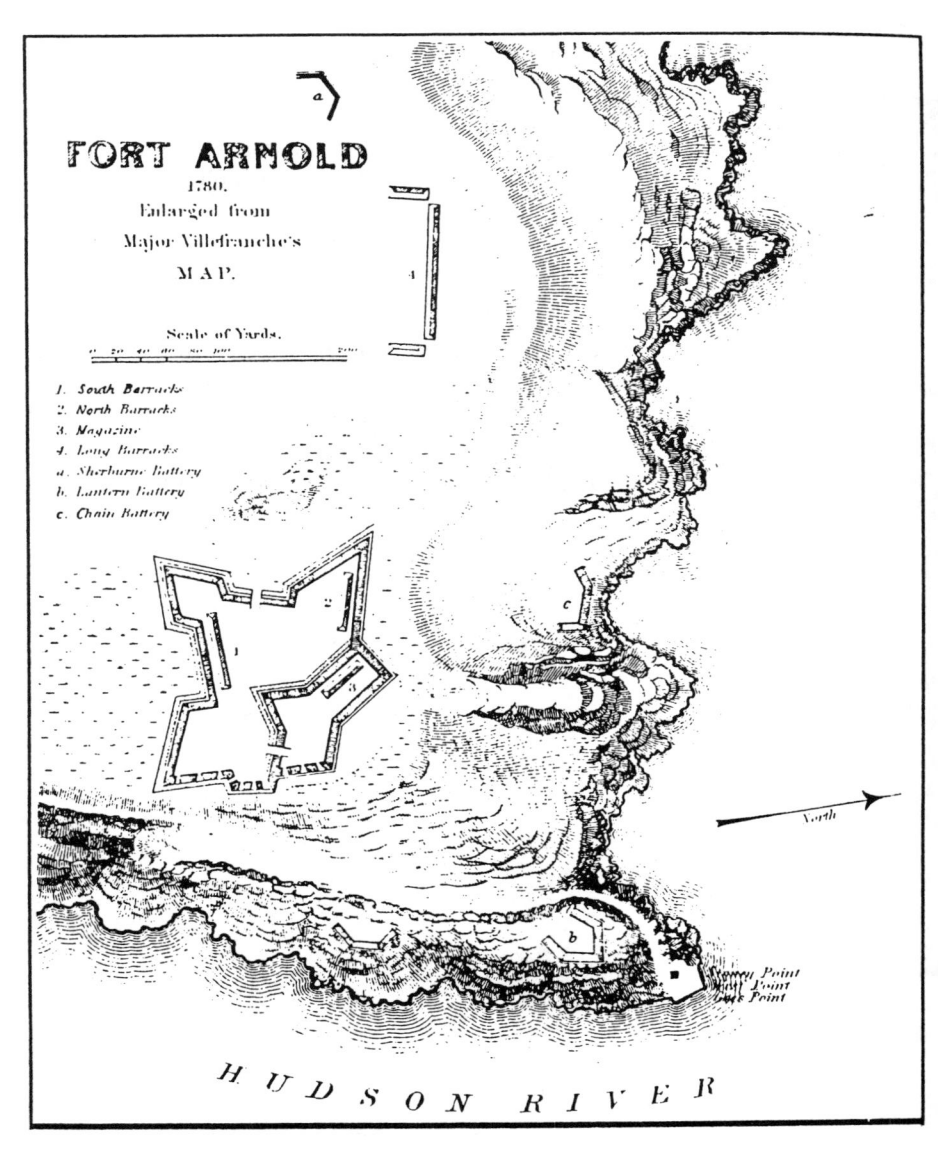

The citadel at Fort Arnold
Boynton, *History of West Point*

Chapter 12

Record of the Court of Inquiry 1780

Proceedings of a Board of General Officers respecting Major John Andre, Adjutant-General of the British Army, September 29th, 1780, Tappan, New York,

Present: Major-General Greene, President
Major-General Lord Stirling, Major-General St. Clair, Major-General the Marquis la Fayette, Major-General Howe, Major-General the Baron von Steuben, Brigadier General Parson, Brigadier General Knox, Brigadier General Glover, Brigadier General Patterson, Brigadier General Hand, Brigadier General Starke, John Lawrence, Judge-Advocate General

Major Andre was brought before the Board and the following letter was read:

"Gentlemen: Major Andre, Adjutant General to the British Army, came within our lines in the assumed character of John Anderson, and was taken in a disguised habit with a pass under a feigned name and with the enclosed papers concealed upon him.

"Hearing of Major Andre's capture, the late Major General Arnold embarked in a barge and proceeded down the river under a flag to the *Vulture* ship-of-war, which lay at some miles below Stony and Verplanck's Points. I enclose the letter he wrote me from aboard the *Vulture*.

"After a careful examination you will be pleased to report a precise state of Major Andre's case together with your opinion of the light in which he ought to be considered and the punishment that ought to be inflicted. The Judge-Advocate will assist in the examination. He has sundry other papers, relative to this matter, which he will lay before the Board. I have the honor to be, gentlemen,
Your most obedient humble servant,
G. Washington"

General Greene obliged the court with a reading of Arnold's letter from the *Vulture*, dated September 25, 1780:

"Sir — The heart is conscious of its own rectitude though it cannot palliate what the world may censure as wrong. I have ever acted from a principle of love to my country since the commencement of the present unhappy contest; the same principle actuates my present conduct, though it may seem inconsistent to the world, which seldom judges right of any man's action.

"Too often have I experienced the ingratitude of my country to ask a favor for myself. But from the known humanity of your Excellency, I am induced to ask your protection of Mrs. Arnold. She is innocent as an angel and incapable of doing wrong. I beg she be permitted to return to her family in Philadelphia or come to me as she chooses. I request the enclosed letter be delivered to Mrs. Arnold and she be permitted to write me.
B. Arnold

"N.B. In justice to the gentlemen of my family, Colonel Varick and Major Franks, I am honor bound to declare that they, as well as Joshua Smith, Esq. (who I know is suspected) are totally ignorant of any transactions of mine that are believed injurious to the public."

Record of the Court of Inquiry 1780

Greene: Gentlemen, we are convened as a court of inquiry empowered to render an opinion only. [to Andre] You are Major Andre, subject of the letter General Washington has directed to this court?

Andre: I am, sir.

Greene: If your case is as stated, will you ease the burden of this court by confessing your guilt?

Andre: While I deny nothing in General Washington's statement, the whole truth is contained in the letter I sent his Excellency upon my capture.

Greene: Will the Judge-Advocate read the letter?

Lawrence: The letter is dated Salem, September 24, 1780:

"Sir — I beg your Excellency will be persuaded that I speak to vindicate my fame, not to solicit security. Having arranged an interview on neutral ground, I came up on the *Vulture* man-of-war, and was fetched by a boat from the shore to the beach. After the interview, I was told the approach of day would prevent my return, and that I must be concealed till the next night. I was in my regimentals.

"Against my intention, I was conducted within one of your posts. Thus a prisoner, I had the duty to escape. To this end I quitted my uniform. Conducted to neutral ground, beyond armed parties, I was left to press for New York. Thus was I betrayed into the vile condition of an enemy in disguise.

"May I request that I be branded with nothing dishonorable as no motive could be mine but the service of my King and as I was involuntarily an imposter. The person in your possession is Major John Andre, Adjutant General of the British Army.

"I take the liberty to mention some American gentlemen on parole in Charleston who engaged in conspiracy against us. They might be exchanged for me or be effected by my treatment."

185

Greene: You are free, Major Andre, to contest anything said. This Board desires that you be at liberty to reply or not as your judgment dictates.

Lawrence: Major Andre, you admit that on the evening of the twenty-second, you passed King's Ferry between our posts of Stony and Verplanck's Points dressed in a hat and coat procured after you landed from the *Vulture*, that you were proceeding to New York and were taken near Tarrytown on Saturday the twenty-third about nine in the morning? And that secret papers were found in your boots?... Take your time, Major Andre. Do not suffer your feelings to be embarrassed. But I caution you to be certain in your response, for you stand in great peril.

Greene: I also exhort you, Sir, to preserve your presence of mind. You may take exception to anything the Judge Advocate has stated, but I add to his caution that you weigh well what you say.

Andre: May I rehearse again the events presented by the Judge Advocate? I shall try to relieve the repetition with facts he neglected and correct those I find mistaken.

Greene: Proceed.

Andre: After speaking with General Arnold, I accompanied him on horse to a house I thought in neutral ground. On the way we passed a guard and I hesitated, having Sir Henry Clinton's instruction not to go within an enemy post.

Lawrence: Did you refuse to enter the American lines?

Andre: I wish it were so. But there seemed nothing I could do except follow General Arnold. In the morning he quitted me, after directing that I put the incriminating papers between my stockings and feet. I already had the gist of them in mind from our interview on neutral ground.

Lawrence: These papers?

The following papers were laid before the Board and shown to Major Andre:

A pass from General Arnold to John Anderson.
Artillery orders, September 5, 1780

Estimate of force at W.P. and dependencies.
Estimate of numbers manning works at W.P.
Return of ordnance at W.P.
Remarks on works at W.P.
Copy of matters discussed at council of war,
Tappan, 6th of September, 1780

Lawrence: These are the papers found in your boots the morning you were taken?
Andre: Except the pass from General Arnold. It was not concealed in my boots.
Lawrence: Even if these papers were not discovered but had been memorized, Major Andre, their contents would still be gained by stealth... Please continue.
Andre: Before leaving me, General Arnold suggested I might cross the river and go back by land, but I was much against it. I thought it was settled that in the way I came I was to return. To my great mortification, my host was determined to carry me by the other route, by land.
Lawrence: By host, you refer not to the late Arnold but Mr. Joshua Smith, at whose house you had spent the first night ashore?
Andre: May I continue? At the decline of the sun we set out on horse, passing King's Ferry, and came to Crompound where a party of militia stopped us. We were advised to remain for the night, which we did. Coming to Pine Bridge the next morning, my companion —
Lawrence: Mr. Smith?... Proceed.
Andre: At the bridge, my companion said he must part with me, as Cowboys infested the road thenceforward. Cowboys being banditti inclined to the British side, I rode on, feeling quite safe. It was in the neighborhood of Tarrytown, beyond the ground described as dangerous, where I was taken by three Skinners, banditti of American persuasion. They rifled me and discovering the papers, made me a prisoner.

Lawrence: For the record, the "banditti" referred to are John Paulding, David Williams and Isaac Van Wort, the selfless irregulars who refused to release the prisoner notwithstanding the liberal reward he offered. True, Major Andre?
Andre: I offered my two watches and they took them. I had nothing more to give.
Lawrence: Haven't you omitted something?
Andre: In my possession?
Lawrence: In your testimony. You fail to mention that you changed dress within an enemy's post.
Andre: My letter to General Washington states that I quitted my uniform.
Lawrence: Can you amplify?
Andre: I was forced to change my dress in spite of Sir Henry Clinton's order forbidding it.
Lawrence: Forced? At the late General Arnold's insistence?... Again I hope you feel no pressure to answer... Did you cross the American lines under an assumed name?
Andre: General Arnold knew me as Major John Andre.
Lawrence: And Mr. Smith?
Andre: If you will pardon me, Sir, I must request that I not be asked anything that does not immediately relate to myself and that I be excused from accusing any other.
Lawrence: I respect Major Andre's firmness and sensibility as I appreciate his candor. You say you intended to meet Arnold and possibly lodge in a place of safety?
Andre: Yes.
Lawrence: For how long?
Andre: Until the next night.
Lawrence: Then you intended to spend the night at a house within American posts?
Andre: To my dismay, Sir.
Lawrence: Intended to your dismay?
Andre: Not intended. I had to be concealed in a place of safety and had every intention of returning to the *Vulture* as soon as possible.

Lawrence: If you were under General Arnold's protection, why conceal yourself?
Andre: I repeat I had no intention of entering the American posts. The sentry's challenge shocked me. My letter to Colonel Sheldon also demonstrates my desire to remain on neutral ground.
Lawrence: Did you write it under your own name?
Andre: As John Anderson.

A letter to Colonel Elisha Sheldon, dated September 7, 1780, was admitted and read to the Board.

Andre: Please notice that the letter was written from New York under orders of General Clinton and requests permission from Colonel Sheldon in command at North Castle to meet a friend, Mr. Gustavus, *near* the post, that is, on neutral ground.
Lawrence: This Mr. Gustavus is Arnold?
Andre: Yes, a disguise he admitted to Colonel Sheldon. Assumed for the purpose of gathering intelligence.
Lawrence: Arnold told that to Sheldon? He had the gall to say that?... And you were central to the scheme! Yet, Major Andre, you claim you became a spy inadvertently?
Andre: I did not become a spy, not at all. I conducted no such activity. I was caught in unfortunate circumstances. I was crushed to learn I could not go back in my regimentals, the way I came.
Lawrence: Then you were a spy in form only, not in essence, will you admit to that?
Andre: Whatever your definition of a spy, Sir, it does not fit my case. It is rhetoric.
Lawrence: Of what else does a court consist? Rhetoric can hang you!
Andre: I perceive your resolve to do it, Sir.
Lawrence: When you recrossed the American lines on your return, were you carrying General Arnold's pass made out to John Anderson?

Andre: Yes.
Lawrence: This pass?
Andre: Yes.
Lawrence: "Permit Mr. John Anderson to pass the guards to the White Plains or below if he chooses. He is on public business by my direction, B. Arnold. M. Gen'l." And under that name you left the *Vulture*?
Andre: On board I was Major Andre. Ashore I assumed the name Anderson for the sake of General Arnold.
Lawrence: Perhaps you will tell the Board, did you leave the *Vulture* under a flag of truce?
Andre: If I had come ashore under that sanction, I might certainly have returned under it.
Lawrence: You would say, then, it was impossible to assume a flag?
Andre: I would say it was impossible to suppose I had come ashore under that sanction.
Lawrence: Then you admit letters from Colonel Beverly Robinson of the *Vulture* on September 25, and from General Clinton on September 26 make false claims?

The following letters were read and admitted into evidence:

"I must inform you that Major Andre, Adjutant General of his Majesty's Army in America, went up with a flag at the request of General Arnold and had his permit to return. Under these circumstances he cannot be detained without the greatest violation of flags. It is contrary to the custom and usage of nations. Every step Major Andre took was by the advice and direction of General Arnold, even that of assuming a feigned name. General Clinton desires his immediate return.
Colonel Beverly Robinson, Loyal Americans."

"Sir — I have the honor to inform your Excellency that I permitted Major Andre to go to Major General Arnold at the particular request of that officer. A flag of truce was sent to

receive Major Andre and a pass granted for his return. I have no doubt but your Excellency will immediately direct that this officer be returned to my orders in New York.
Lt. Gen. Clinton, Commander of the British Army."

General Clinton enclosed the following letter received of the late General Arnold aboard the *Vulture*, September 25:

"Sir Henry Clinton — I apprehend a few hours must return Major Andre to your Excellency as that officer is assuredly under the protection of a flag of truce I sent him. At the time I commanded West Point and had an undoubted right to send my flag for Major Andre. I gave him confidential papers to deliver to your Excellency. I also directed he use the feigned name John Anderson, and gave him a passport to go to the White Plains on his way to New York.

"This officer cannot therefore fail of being immediately returned to your Excellency."

Lawrence: These letters stress the point that you went up with a flag, Major Andre, and were under orders of the American general at all times ashore. But you have testified to the contrary, that you did not at any time consider yourself under the protection of a flag, nor of the late general —
Steuben: From his own mouth, condemned!
Greene: Quiet! Will the general withhold?
Lawrence: — but rather that you were a prisoner dutybound to escape. Major Andre, is that your testimony?
Andre: It is what I wrote General Washington. Yes.
Lawrence: Did you consider yourself a private individual when you came ashore or a British officer?
Andre: I was in uniform and esteemed myself to be what indeed I am, a British officer.
Greene: Did Mr. Smith force you into disguise as you lay concealed in his house?... Major Andre?

Lawrence: The prisoner wishes to incriminate no one, General Greene. He therefore objects to the form of your question. Ask rather if the disguise was against his wishes.

Greene: Will Major Andre answer that question?

Andre: I donned that coat and hat with great mortification.

Greene: Were you obeying an order from Arnold?

Andre: It was found necessary in order to return through the American lines.

Greene: Why? You had Arnold's pass?

Andre: I must confess the moment's pressure caused poor judgment.

Greene: Lost your head?

Andre: My desire to reach British lines was paramount.,

Lawrence: As I understand, you obtained the papers found in your boots while at Smith's house?

Andre: If you will pardon me, I said *a* house, I did not say whose.

Greene: Such questions are more appropriate for Smith's court of inquiry, Mr. Lawrence.

Lawrence: Were these papers forced upon you? Placed in your boot by order of General Arnold?

Andre: He was in command of the district where I was engaged.

Lawrence: No officer is obliged to obey an enemy's order. But doesn't it appear absurd? I mean to acknowledge an order that leads to your destruction? Or respect a flag issued to cover suborning of treason?

Andre: I do not wish to speculate, Sir. I have denied the line on which the Board is trying me — as a spy. But I see my defense is not taken seriously, though I have frankly acknowledged all the facts relating to myself while guarding against whatever may incriminate others. No choice remains to me but to have the evidence operate with the court as it will.

Lawrence: The court is impressed with your candor and firmness.

Greene: We all appreciate Major Andre's sensibility, and we are grateful that he shields our sentiments from emotional appeals.

Knox: The dignity of his conduct has inspired tenderness for his situation throughout the American Army.

Stueben: If prisoner will change story and say like Clinton and Arnold, yes, I am under flag, then —

Andre: Then I would lose the respect just displayed, which ought to tell you I am not an ordinary knave trying to save his neck.

Greene: We understand you wish to be spared but not at the expense of honor.... Have you concluding thoughts for the Board?

Andre: I assert for the court's conscience that I am not a spy but Sir Henry Clinton's deputy. History supports me. I recall from my military schooling at Göttingen that among the laws of nations, an officer under the sanction of an enemy's commander is guaranteed personal safety even if his purpose is treacherous. Though I admit to no flag, I did have General Arnold's sanction, and should have been returned.

I see my mission in a humane light, as aiming to end this foul war, but you have pressed another interpretation upon it. Let me say that even treacherous business does not contravene the general military understanding that war justifies all military strategies. My strategy was pursued in discharge of my duty. It was to receive the terms and conditions of a subject returning to the allegiance of his sovereign, which might further the rescue of two countries from the horrors of continued bloodshed.

I respectfully submit these thoughts to the Court's consideration and extend my gratitude for the Board's generosity and indulgence.

No witnesses being called, the examination of Major Andre was concluded and the prisoner remanded into custody.

The Board, having considered the evidence and circumstances respecting Major Andre, and his confession, report to his Excellency, the Commander-in-Chief, the following facts:

First, That Major Andre came on shore from the *Vulture* sloop of war in the night of the twenty-first of September on an interview with the late General Arnold in a private and secret manner.

Second, That he changed his dress within our lines and under a feigned name and a disguised habit passed our works at Stony and Verplanck's Points the evening of the twenty-second of September, being then on his way to New York. When taken at Tarrytown, he had in his possession several papers which contained intelligence for the enemy.

Having maturely considered these facts, the Board reports to his Excellency General Washington, that Major Andre, Adjutant General to the British Army, ought to be considered a spy from the enemy and that, agreeable to the laws and usage of nations, it is their opinion, he ought to suffer death.
                Nathanael Greene, Major-General
                      President for the Board

Addenda
    Copy of letter from Major Andre to Sir Henry Clinton, K.B. etc.

Tappan, Sept. 29, 1780

Sir — I have obtained General Washington's permission to send you this letter to remove from your breast any misconception. The events of coming within an enemy's post and changing my dress where as contrary to my own intentions as they were to your orders; and the route I took to return was imposed upon me. I am tranquil in mind and prepared for any fate.

With all the warmth of my heart, I give thanks for your Excellency's profuse kindness; and I send the most earnest wishes for your welfare that a faithful, affectionate, and respectful attendant can frame.

I have a mother and three sisters to whom the value of my commission would be an object. It is needless to be more explicit on this subject. I am persuaded of your Excellency's goodness. I receive the greatest attention from his Excellency, General Washington, and his officers.

    With most respectful attachment,
     John Andre, Adjutant General

  Copy of letter to his Excellency Sir Henry Clinton. (Above letter was enclosed):

Headquarters, September 30, 1780

Sir — To answer your Excellency's letter of the 26th: From the proceedings, it is evident Major Andre was employed in the execution of a measure very foreign to the purposes of a flag of truce. Further, in the course of his examination, this gentlemen confessed with the greatest candor,
    Your most obedient and humble servant,
     G. Washington

  Copy of unsigned fragment included with the letters above:

Lt. General Henry Clinton, Sir — There is no time to be lost. Your justice and friendship should demand Andre for Arnold. Major Andre's character and accomplishment are much admired though an enemy's. Arnold ought to be the victim.

Copy of letter to his Excellency General Washington:

New York, September 30, 1780

Sir — From your Excellency's letter of this date,I am persuaded the Board of General Officers cannot have been rightly informed of all the circumstances. It is of the highest moment to humanity that your Excellency should be perfectly apprised of this matter before you put the Board's judgment into execution.

For this reason, I send his Excellency Lieutenant General Robertson, Royal Governor of New York, and two other gentlemen to give you a true state of facts and declare to you my sentiments and resolutions. They will set out tomorrow aboard the *Greyhound* schooner as early as the wind and tide will permit and wait near Dobb's Ferry for your safe conduct to meet your Excellency or such persons as you may appoint.
    Your Excellency's obedient and humble servant
        H. Clinton

P.S. The Hon. Andrew Elliot, esq., Lieutenant Governor, and the Hon. William Smith, chief Justice of this province, will attend his Excellency Lieutenant General Robertson, Royal Governor.

    Copy of undated and unsigned letter surreptitiously delivered to Major Andre by his servant Peter Luane who was permitted to bring the prisoner clean linens, regimentals and boots.

Andre — God knows I feel for you in the present situation. I dare hope you'll soon be returned from it. They haven't a legal pin and wouldn't dare carry out the threat. But I am chagrined to find one legal son-of-a-bitch in my own family who thinks otherwise. I'm sending a delegation to give Washington the true state of affairs. They'll surely outweigh the Board's opinion.

General Arnold has received a letter from his wife who blames you for the horrendous blunder. The distracted woman hopes to join her husband when her baby is secure. She set out for her father's house in Philadelphia, which cast General Arnold into deep depression. In that state he offered his own person in exchange for yours. I said the offer did him great honor but if Andre were my brother I could not consent to it.

He talked wildly then of rescuing Major Andre when the whole royal army proved helpless. Though he might perish he would be remembered not as a traitor but a hero after his misguided countrymen betrayed him. He needed assurance that I would provide substantial benefits for his family.

General Order of the Day, October 1, 1780
To examine new evidence offered by British General Henry Clinton, the execution of Major John Andre is delayed. It is rescheduled for precisely 12:00 on the morrow, a battalion of 80 files from each wing to attend. G. Washington.

Copy of letter from Gov. Robertson to Gen. Washington:

Greyhound Schooner, Flag of Truce

Dobb's Ferry, October 2, 1780

Sir — Because we must avoid any misunderstanding in a matter of so much consequence, I put into writing the substance of what I said to General Greene.

Not being military, Lt. Governor Elliot and Chief Justice Smith were excluded from the meeting. General Greene asked that we speak only as private gentleman, not officially, as "an acknowledged spy admits no discussion."

I agreed that his facts correspond with the evidence, but insisted he admits a conclusion that does not follow. The change of clothes and name were ordered by General Arnold, to whom Andre had come under a flag and whose direction he obeyed according to the laws of nations and war.

General Greene answered, "But Andre testified he had not come under a flag. Andre is a man of honor. Arnold is a traitor. Whom should we believe?"

I responded, "Whatever Major Andre in his confused state may have uttered, the conditions were those of a flag," and I suggested that disinterested gentlemen who know the laws of war and nations might be asked their opinion on the subject and mentioned Generals Knyphausen and Rochambeau. "They are citizens of the world, alien to both countries. Their judgment would be close to humanity."

Major Andre has a great share of Sir Henry's esteem, I told General Greene. "If you permit him to return with me, I will engage to set at liberty any person your Excellency names." General Greene suggested that one already at liberty be delivered. I reminded him a deserter is never given up.

Sir Henry Clinton, I added, has never put to death any person for a breach of the rules of war though he had and now has many in his power. We wait aboard the *Greyhound* for your response.
    Your Excellency's most obedient servant,
        James Robertson

    Accompanying note to his Excellency General Washington, undated:

Sir — If Andre suffers, I call heaven and earth to witness that you will be answerable for the torrent of blood spilt in consequence.
    Your most obedient and very humble servant,
        B. Arnold

    Copy of letter to his Excellency General Washington:
        Tappan, October 1, 1780

Record of the Court of Inquiry 1780

Sir — Bouy'd above the terror of death by consciousness of a life devoted to honorable pursuits, I trust that the request I make to soften my last moments will not be rejected. Sympathy towards a soldier will surely induce your Excellency to adapt the mode of my death to the feelings of a man of honor.

Let me hope, Sir, that if aught in my character impresses you, if aught in my misfortunes marks me as the victim of policy and not of resentment, I shall not die on a gibbet.
Your Excellency's most obedient and humble servant,
John Andre, Adj. Gen to the British Army.

Major Andre was executed on the gibbet at twelve o'clock on the second of October, 1780. The practice and usage of war were against his request, and made the indulgence he solicited inadmissible.

Published by Order of Congress, Oct. 7, 1780

Charles Thomson, Secretary

200

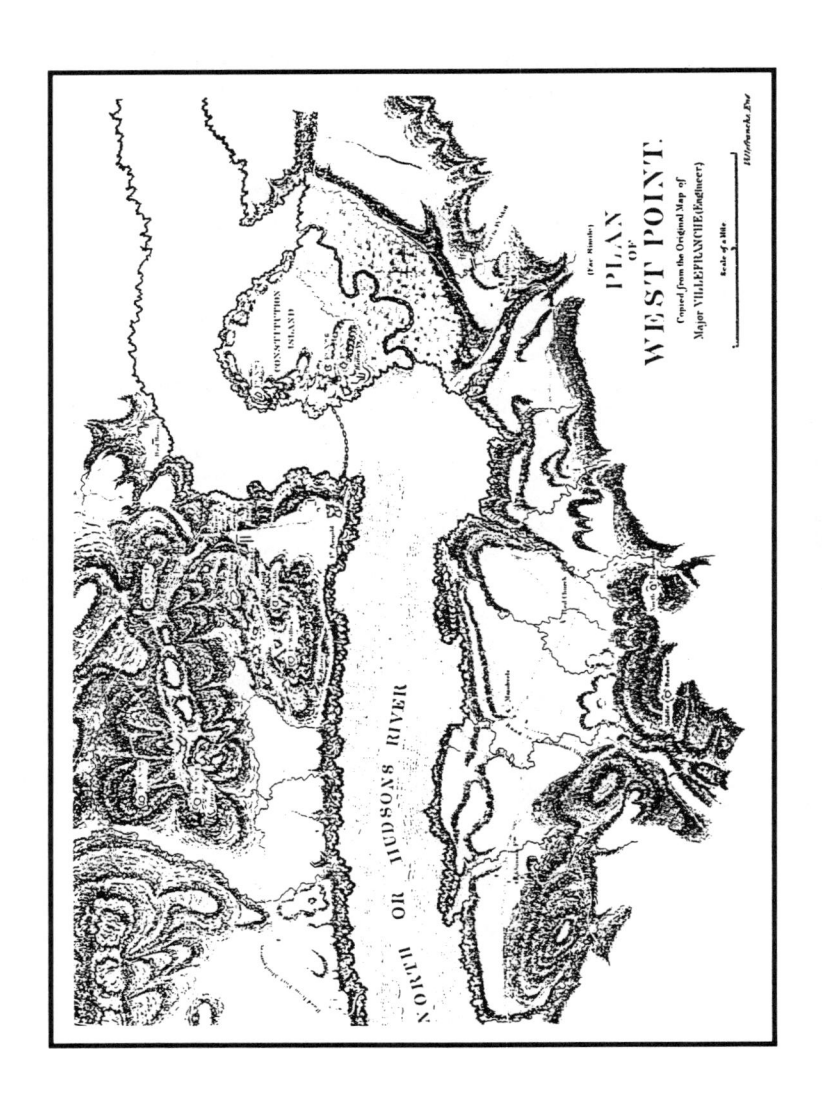

Bibliography

Abbatt, William, *The Crisis of the American Revolution*, New York, 1899.
Abbott, Wilber C., *New York in the American Revolution*, New York, 1929.
Adams, Randolph G. "Tragedy of Arnold Revealed," *New York Sunday Times*, April 11, 1926.
Andre, John, *Journal: Operations of the British Army, June 1777 to November 1788*, Tarrytown, N.Y. 1930.
—"Narrative of the Siege of St. Johns," *Report of the Public Archives of Canada, 1914-15*, pp. 18-25.
—Particulars of the Mischianza," *Gentleman's Magazine*, XLVIII, 1778, pp. 353-57.
Almond, John. *The Remembrancer*, vol 5, London, 1775-84.
Arnold, Isaac N., *The Life of Benedict Arnold*, Chicago, 1880.
Ashmun, Margaret, *The Singing Swan, Anna Seward and Her Acquaintances*, New Haven, 1931.
"Authentic Account of that Greatly Lamented Officer, Major John Andre," *Political Magazine,* II, London, pp. 171-73.
Bacon, Edgar Mayhew, *The Capture of Major Andre*, N.P. 1930.
Bakeless, John, *Turncoats, Traitors and Heroes*, New York, 1959.
Barck, Oscar T. *New York City During the War for Independence.* New York, 1931.
Biddle, Charles J. "The Case of Major Andre," *Memoirs of the Historical Society of Pennsylvania*, vol II, pp. 319-416.
Bolton, Robert, *A History of the County of Westchester from its First Settlement to its Present Time*, New York, 1848.
Bradford, Gamaliel, *Damaged Souls.* Boston, 1923.
—"Wife of the Traitor." *Harper's Magazine*, vol 151.

Boudinot, Elias, *Journal of the Events in the Revolution*. Philadelphia, 1894.
Boylan, Brian Richard. *Benedict Arnold, The Dark Eagle*. New York, 1973.
Boynton, Edward C. *History of West Point*, New York, 1871.
Burnett, Edmund, ed. *Letters of Members of the Continental Congress*, Washington, D.C., 1921-36.
Calvert, George Henry, *Arnold and Andre*, rpt. Tarrytown, N.Y. 1923.
Campbell, Charles A., "Bibliography of Major Andre," *Magazine of American History, VIII, pp. 61-72*.
Chapman, John Jay, *The Treason and Death of Benedict Arnold: A Play for Greek Theatre*, Norwood, Ma. 1910.
Chester, Joseph Lemuel. "Some Particulars Respecting the Family of Major John Andre," *Proceedings of the Massachusetts Historical Society*, 1875-76.
Clinton, Sir Henry, *The American Rebellion*, William B. Willcox, ed. New Haven, 1954.
—*Papers*. Clement Library, University of Michigan.
Cope, Gilbert, *A Record of the Cope Family*. Philadelphia, 1851.
Dawson, Henry B. ed. *Papers Concerning the Capture and Detention of Major John Andre*, Yonkers, N.Y. 1866.
—*Record of the Trial of Joshua Hett Smith*, Morrisania, N.Y. 1866.
Decker, Malcolm, *Benedict Arnold: Son of the Havens*, New York, 1932.
—*Ten Days of Infamy*, New York, 1969.
Diary of Grace Growden Galloway, rpt. New York, 1971.
Dumezil, George, *The Destiny of the Warrior*, Chicago, 1970.
Edgeworth, Richard Lovell. *Memoirs*. London, 1844.
Fitzpatrick, John C. ed. *The Writings of George Washington from the Original Manuscript Sources, 1745-1799*. Library of Congress, Washington, D.C., 1931-44.
Flexner, James T. *The Traitor and the Spy, Benedict Arnold and John Andre*. New York, 1953.
Force, Peter, ed. *American Archives*, Library of Congress, Washington, D.C. 1837-53.

Bibliography

Ford, Corey. *A Peculiar Service*, Boston, 1965.
Gessner, Robert. *Treason*. New York, 1944.
Gocek, Matilda. *Benedict Arnold: A Reader's Guide and Bibliography*. Monroe, N.Y. 1973.
Hamilton, Alexander. *Writings*. edited by Henry Cabot Lodge.12 vols. New York, 1904.
Haswell, Jock. *British Military Intelligence*. London, 1973.
Hatch, Robert McConnell. *Major John Andre, A Gallant in Spy's Clothing*. Boston, 1986.
Henry, John J. *Account of Arnold's Campaign Against Quebec*. Albany, 1877.
Hensel, W.U. *Major John Andre as a Prison of War at Lancaster, Pa., 1775-76*. Lancaster, Pa., 1904.
Hopkins, Mary Alden. *Dr. Johnson's Lichfield*. New York, 1952.
Jones, Thomas. *History of New York During the Revolutionary War*. New York, 1879.
Koke, Richard J. *Accomplice in Treason, Joshua Hett Smith and the Arnold Conspiracy*. New York, 1973.
Lawrence, J.W. *Footprints or Incidents in the Early History of New Brunswick*. St. John's, 1883.
Leake, Isaac Q. *Memoir of the Life and Times of General John Lamb*. New York, 1875.
Lengyel, Cornel Adam. *I, Benedict Arnold, The Anatomy of Treason*. New York, 1960.
Lossing, Benson J. *The Pictorial Field-Book of the Revolution*. New York, 1859-60.
Metzger, Charles H. *The Quebec Act, A Primary Cause of the Revolution*. New York, 1936.
Minutes of the Court of Inquiry upon the Case of Major John Andre with Accompanying Documents. Albany, 1865.
Montressor, John. "Journals," edited by G.D. Skull *New York Historical Society Collections*. 1881.
Moore, Frank. *Diary of the American Revolution from Newspapers and Original Documents*. New York, 1858.
Morris, Robert. *Morris, Arnold, and Battersby*. London, 1782.
Paine, Lauren. *Benedict Arnold, Hero and Traitor*. London, 1965.

Paine, Thomas. "A Crisis Extraordinary," *Gentlemen's Magazine.* LXIV (August 1794), p.685.
Parton, James. *Life and Times of Benjamin Franklin.* New York, 1864.
Pearson, Hesketh. *The Swan of Lichfield, A Selection from the Correspondence of Anna Seward.* London, 1936.
Proceedings of a Board of General Officers Held by Order of His Excellency Gen. Washington Respecting Major John Andre, Adjutant General of the British Army. Philadelphia, 1780.
Riedesel von, Baroness. *Letters and Journals Relating to the War of the American Revolution.* Wm. Stone, trans. Albany, 1867.
Sabine, Lorenzo. *Biographical Sketches of Loyalists of the American Revolution.* 2 vols. 1864. rpt. New York, 1966.
Sargent, Winthrop. *The Life and Career of Major John Andre.* Boston, 1861.
Scott, S.H. *The Exemplary Mr. Day.* London, 1935.
Sellars, Charles. *B. Arnold: Proud Warrior.* New York, 1930.
Seward, Anna. *Letters.* London, 1811.
—*Monody on Major Andre, to which are added Letters Addressed to her by Major Andre.* Lichfield, England, 1781.
Simcoe, James Graves. *Military Journal: A History of the Operations of a Partisan Corps Called the Queen's Rangers.* New York, 1844.
Smith, Joshua Hett. *An Authentic Narrative of the Causes Which Led to the Death of Major Andre.* London, 1808.
Sparks, Jared. *Correspondence of the American Revolution.* Boston, 1853.
—*The Life and Treason of Benedict Arnold.* Boston, 1853.
Stimpson, Frederick J. *My Story: Being the Memoirs of Benedict Arnold.* New York, 1917.
Stokes, Richard Leroy. *Benedict Arnold.* New York, 1941.
Sullivan, Edward Dean. *Benedict Arnold, Military Racketeer.* New York, 1932.
Syme, Ronald. *Benedict Arnold, Traitor of the Revolution.* New York, 1970.

Tallmadge, Benjamin. *Memoirs.* Edited by Henry P. Johnson. New York, 1904.
—*Tallmadge-Arnold Letters.* Library of Congress.
Tillotson, Harry Standard. *The Beloved Spy.* Caldwell, Idaho, 1948.
—*The Exquisite Exile: The Life and Fortune of Mrs. Benedict Arnold.* Boston, 1932.
Todd, Charles Burr. *The Real Benedict Arnold.* New York, 1903.
Vail, Philip. *Twisted Saber.* New York, 1963.
Van de Water, Frederick. *The Reluctant Rebel.* New York, 1948.
Van Doren, Carl. *Secret History of the American Revolution.* New York, 1941.
Van Tyne, Claude H. *Loyalists in the American Revolution.* New York, 1902.
Vivian, Francis St. Clair. "Capture and Death of Major Andre," *History Today* VII, no. 12, (December 1957).
—"John Andre as a Young Officer," *Journal of the Society for Army Historical Research.* XL, nos. 161 and 162 (March, June 1962).
Walker, Lewis Burd. "The Life of Margaret Shippen, Wife of Benedict Arnold," *Pennsylvania Magazine of History and Biography.* XXIV-XXVI, (1900-1902).
Wallace, Willard M. *Traitorious Hero: The Life and Fortunes of Benedict Arnold.* New York, 1954.
Watson, John F. *Annals of Philadelphia and Pennsylvania in the Olden Time.* Philadelphia, 1877.
Willcox, William B. *Portrait of a General: Sir Henry Clinton and the War of Independence.* New York, 1964.

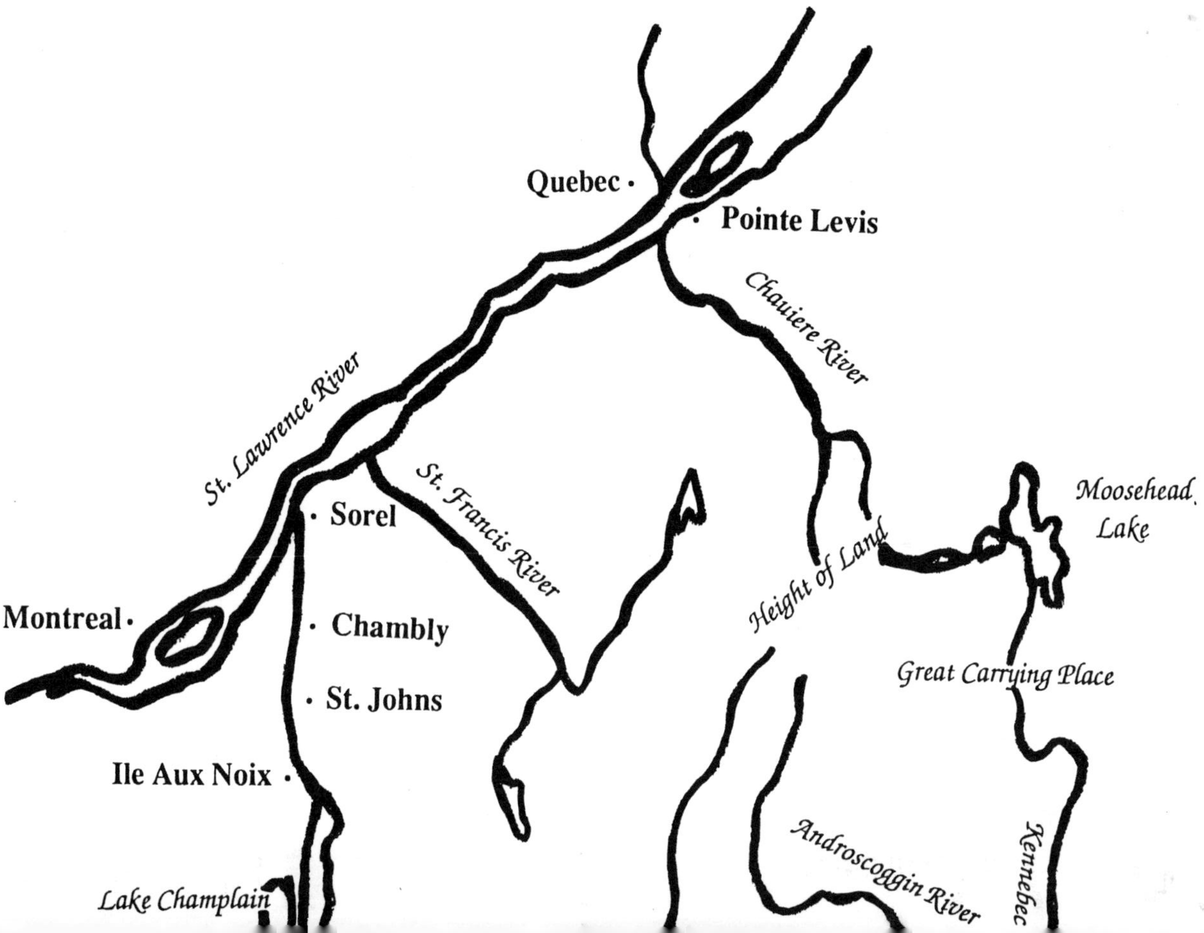
Quebec
Pointe Levis
Chauiere River
St. Lawrence River
St. Francis River
Moosehead Lake
Height of Land
Sorel
Montreal
Chambly
St. Johns
Great Carrying Place
Ile Aux Noix
Androscoggin River
Kennebec
Lake Champlain